in my neighborhood celebrating wisconsin cities

an anthology of essays, poems and photographs
looking at the cities of Wisconsin—
their past, their present and the promise for their future

edited by andrea dearlove and mary mcintyre

Prairie Oak Press
Madison, Wisconsin

First edition, first printing
Copyright © 2000 by 1000 Friends of Wisconsin

Published by Prairie Oak Press for 1000 Friends of Wisconsin

Prairie Oak Press
821 Prospect Place
Madison, Wisconsin 53703

1000 Friends of Wisconsin
16 North Carroll Street
Madison, Wisconsin 53703
Tel. 608 259-1000
www.1kfriends.org

Designed by Nancy Zucker, Madison, Wisconsin
Printed in Korea
Distributed by Prairie Oak Press

Library of Congress Cataloging-in-Publication Data

In my neighborhood : celebrating Wisconsin cities : an anthology of essays, poems, and
photographs looking at cities of Wisconsin, their past, their present and the promise
for the future / edited by Andrea Dearlove and Mary McIntyre.—1st ed.
        p. cm.
    ISBN 1-879483-76-9 (pbk)
    1. Wisconsin—History, Local—Miscellanea. 2. Cities and
towns—Wisconsin—Miscellanea. 3. Wisconsin—Social life and customs—Miscellanea 4.
City and town life—Wisconsin—Miscellanea. I. Dearlove, Andrea, 1968- II McIntyre,
Mary, 1960-

F581.5 .I5 2000
977—dc21
                                                        00-049195

acknowledgements

As is the case with many non-profit projects, this book was not the product of one or two people. This book was made possible quite simply due to the contributions and patience of many wonderful people.

First and foremost we owe a great debt of gratitude to all of the authors, poets and photographers who contributed their work to this book because they love the cities they call home and agreed with us that these urban places deserved some overdue affection.

For their assistance with soliciting submissions, we thank Kurt Chandler from *Milwaukee Magazine*, Anne Kingsbury and Karl Gartung from Woodland Pattern Book Center, John McLean from the John Michael Kohler Arts Center, photographer Gerry Emmerich and Stuart Levitan.

For their contributions of ideas and moral support we thank Debra Kay Vest, Emily Kort, Paul Haig, Paul Dearlove, Mike Maierle, Mike Magnuson, Kathy Bero and Dennis Boyer.

For their advice and wisdom in designing and distributing the book, we thank Nancy Zucker and Jerry Minnich.

For having the idea to publish this book and dreaming up the title, we heartily thank Dave Cieslewicz.

Finally, the printing of this anthology would not have been possible without the generous and anonymous contributions of members of the 1000 Friends of Wisconsin Board of Directors—thank you for your confidence in and excitement for this project—and for enabling us to see it through!

Student essays appear thanks to a 1999 grant from the Wisconsin Environmental Education Board.

Two years ago, 1000 Friends published its first book, *A Place to Which We Belong*. Through this book we celebrated Wisconsin's open spaces—its farms and forests, its prairies and wetlands, its bluffs and valleys. Some of Wisconsin's best writers were enlisted to reflect on the undeniable impact that open landscapes have in shaping our impressions, our communities, and even our personalities. These cherished places define the rural character of a state that takes pride in its abundant natural resources.

There are many books on the shelves of libraries and bookstores about the pull and magic inherent in Wisconsin's "natural" areas. But you will find far fewer discussing the role and importance of our cities. During the development of this book, the reasons for this scarcity became apparent. We had hoped to devote one of the anthology's sections to young people writing about their urban neighborhoods. We solicited essays from highschools throughout the state, explaining clearly the book's goal: celebrating Wisconsin's urban experience. To our surprise, many of the essays we received recounted the wonders of camping and playing in rural surroundings. (Happily, two of the essays we received were wonderful accounts of urban life and you will find them at the end of the first chapter.)

What is it about our cities that we refuse to embrace? Why do images of crime-ridden neighborhoods and poor-quality schools predominate? Are all our widely held suppositions about cities true? Are our one-dimensional perspectives of them fair or accurate? And if they are—does that mean the best option is to leave our cities for the country? Or do we have other alternatives that will not only improve the quality of life in our cities but also protect the open spaces for which we care so deeply?

The talented authors, poets and photographers who have contributed to this anthology remind us of those uniquely urban things that are worth celebrating, as they also address the challenges of urban life. They speak eloquently of the pull and magic of our cities—a pull that is just as critical to shaping our communities and our personalities as the love affair we have with our open spaces.

In this book you will read about many different Wisconsin cities, each essay and poem touching on what the author finds special about his or her urban home. Despite the variety of authors and topics, one theme runs constant: the potential of human contact and human creativity. Ultimately, it is not the buildings, the neighborhoods, the activities that are what truly make cities great—it is instead the significant opportunity for human contact. An opportunity that is only truly available in our cities.

In her book, *The Death and Life of Great American Cities*, Jane Jacobs admitted that to promote density is like "swimming with the sharks." Yet, without density generally—and more specifically, lots of people working synergistically—we would not have our theatres, stadiums, great restaurants, parades, museums, close-knit neighborhoods and architectural wonders. In short, cities—and the densities they allow—stimulate the development of our culture.

There are few who would argue the importance of solitude, of being surrounded by vast open spaces. But we are a social species. It is through interaction with each other that we find common ground, that we remove stereotypes, that we find love, and the inspiration to create great communities.

We hope that this book reminds us all of why cities are so important, and why they deserve recognition and some overdue celebration.

Andrea Dearlove, Director
The 1000 Friends Land Use Institute

In contrast to the self-sustaining environment of the countryside, the order of which is natural or organic, the order of cities relies upon human dynamics. An urban environment evolves through human invention and interaction. Its continued growth and prosperity are a reflection of the efforts of its inhabitants. Our cities are dependent upon our willingness to uphold their vitality, character and sense of community.

The purpose of this volume is to make our readers aware that our cities are far more for us than a set of boundaries we happen to live within. What you'll find here is a variety of voices, views and topics as multi-faceted as the urban landscape itself—descriptions of pace and tempo; explorations of relationships; accounts of customs and traditions; observations of the old coexisting with the new; tributes to our homes, corporations and social institutions.

This highly varied forum includes within its range everything from the introspective, abstract works of poets that elevate a commonplace aspect of urban life to a universal experience, to the discourse of urban planners concerned with re-defining and preserving our cities' attributes. Many of these writings reveal the human growth that occurs through the many roles we play within our neighborhoods, and illustrate what we discover about ourselves through our conventions and routines.

Just as people create cities, cities create people. Our objective is to inspire our readers to take stock in the urban environment that has contributed to forming our identity. This book itself is the result of an act of statewide community. The professors, historians, journalists, poets, educators, students, novelists, playwrights and photographers represented have in common more than just a geographic location. They possess a desire to make known their appreciation for urban living. The contributors who've shared their perceptions and beliefs have done so with humor, with truth, with concern.

Just as we hope our contributors can take pride in the end product of their efforts, we hope that our readers are inspired to become more aware of the beauty and distinction of the cities we inhabit.

Mary McIntyre
Contributing Editor

forewords

acknowledgements

in my neighborhood

photograph, **tom bamberger** 12
living the sweet life, **joe gozdowiak** 13
the kindness of neighbors, **katherine esposito** 15
photograph, **zane williams** 17
a sense of place, **kurt chandler** 18
city lawns, **dave cieslewicz** 19
sunday morning, **bruce taylor** 21
neighbors, **rachel nuetzel** 22
life in my city, **veronica bieganski** 23
photograph, **mary jo walicki** 25

a sense of community

photograph, **brent nicastro** 28
the blue plate special, **eve tai** 29
finding our way back downtown, **jane tappen** 31
photograph, **tim holte** 33
the people you meet, **bill new** 34
the gathering, **marie kohler** 37
talking townie, **john roach** 38
new urbanism comes to wisconsin, **whitney gould** 41
new york city: port of my re-entry, **ben logan** 44
olbrich botanical gardens, **jerry minnich** 47
photograph, **brent nicastro** 49

the city at play

photograph, **henry h. smith** 52
titletown and its packers, **thomas m. olejniczak** 53
the people's park, **bruce murphy** 55
red hot red, the wizard of waukesha, **will kort** 57

photograph, **courtesy of waukesha county museum** 59
untitled, **susan firer** 60
photograph, **henry h. smith** 62
city legs, **william hurrle** 63
civil disobedience by dawn's early light, **vince vukelich** 65
photograph, **thairath khanthavong** 67

city excursions

photograph, **mary jo walicki** 70
urban cool and the city wild: three vignettes, **judith strasser** 71
the cedarburg illusion, **paul hayes** 73
la crosse at a runner's pace, **chris hardie** 75
madison, by peddle and paddle, **mike lvey** 77
photograph, **brent nicastro** 79
retreat, **john fennell** 80
photograph, **henry h. smith** 81
milwaukee morning, **annette craig** 82

city reminiscences

hometown pastiche, **helen padway** 86
photograph, **henry h. smith** 88
a marriage with milwaukee, **c.j. hribal** 89
the commute, **brent goodman** 91
roasting chestnuts, **peggy hong** 92
outside the box, **stephen filmanowicz** 94
photograph, **zane williams** 95
photograph, **tim holte** 96
sunday at st. josaphat's, **julie king** 97
the tin tepee, **lynn shoemaker** 98
photograph, **zane williams** 99

city culture

photograph, **courtesy of harley davidson motor company** 102
the first harley davidson factory in milwaukee: icon for the city, **dr. martin jack rosenblum** 103
photograph, **zane williams** 106

rudy's cornerstone bar and grill, **dennis boyer** 107
green bay's broadway, **tom williams** 109
brady street: the continual traffic of subcultural chic, **mary mcintyre** 111
photograph, **ned luhm** 113
the health department inspector watches her daytime talk shows, **sue blaustein** 114
photograph, **courtesy of john michael kohler arts center** 116
the arts & industry program, **john mclean** 117

cities, past and present

photograph, **colin kloecker** 120
an alliance of cities, **edward j. huck** 121
photograph, **courtesy of sc johnson** 124
the johnson wax administration building, **kristin visser** 125
architectural treasures built of brownstone crown recall the boom times, **claire duquette** 127
cities of the fox river valley, **ellen kort** 129
photograph, **zane williams** 132
stoughton, **tracy will** 133
dasengelflugenhaus—the history of a home, **randolph d. brandt** 136
photograph, **brent nicastro** 139

the role of cities

photograph, **tom bamberger** 142
the wealth of cities—the milwaukee advantage, **mayor john o. norquist** 143
why do we need milwaukee?, **bruce murphy** and **tom bamberger** 148
searching for urban wisconsin, **harvey m. jacobs** 152
photograph, **henry h. smith** 155

epilogue

photograph, **ryan heckel** 158
the old neighborhood, **ray suarez** 159

about the photographers, artists and art work 163

in my neighborhood

tom bamberger girl engaged in street painting

living the sweet life

joe gozdowiak

Every person has a place that defines his childhood, a place where lifelong bonds of friendship are made, a place where he was a kid. For me, that place was Violet's Sweet Shop, nestled on a corner of Milwaukee's South Side. However, the smiling face that was a fixture behind the counter was not Violet, but her husband Casey, and it was by his name that the place was known by the droves of neighborhood kids who were its eager and loyal clientele.

Casey and Violet were obviously familiar with the real estate motto regarding location because they set up shop in a part of the city that would guarantee a steady flow of customers who were more than willing to part with their hard-earned allowance. The sweet shop was located within a block of our elementary school and playground. After all, when finished with a hard day of pounding the books, what better than an ice-cold soda and conversation with classmates, reliving the day's events and deciding what to do that afternoon? Worked up an appetite after a particularly vigorous game of dodge ball at the playground? No problem. Cross the street to Casey's and there awaited never-ending options to satisfy even the most demanding consumer. It was the perfect place to cure whatever ailed you.

One of the attractions of Casey's was its appearance—a Milwaukee bungalow with the lower level converted into the sweet shop. In place of a porch there was simply a concrete stoop, which was infinitely better. The perfect place to sit and indulge in the purchases of the day. Plus, it gave a kid the perfect vantage point to sit and take in what was going on at the playground. It was the best of both worlds—a delectable treat as you relaxed, no need to worry about being left out of the loop of the playground's social circle.

Being kids, a steady means of income was a luxury that we weren't privileged to have. Allowances only go so far. However, at Casey's, complete happiness was yours for a mere dollar. Swedish fish, candy buttons, licorice pipes, army men with plastic parachutes on their backs…you name it, Casey's had it, and all in a kid's price range. Five for a penny, ten for a nickel, the best deal in town. With a dollar, you could forget all the daily hassles of the third grade and lose yourself in the rainbow of colors and choices waiting for you behind the glass cases. Not bad for a buck.

But Casey's wasn't just a place you went to forget your problems; it was the place you went to solve problems. There was a popular game in the neighborhood known simply as "off the wall." The only equipment needed to play was a rubber ball and a garage door, preferably not white, as many of the neighborhood dads would tell you. It was a great alternative for when the playground diamonds were full, or you couldn't round up enough kids for a full game, which was rarely a problem. The rules were simple. The purpose was to bounce the ball off the driveway, ricochet it off the garage door, and attempt to get it on the garage roof behind you, this constituting a home run. With a little practice and a fresh rubber ball, any kid could be a home run king. Summer nights would find us out there, complete with the plastic batting helmets purchased at County Stadium, demonstrating our athletic prowess.

Along with the sweet victory of home runs came the bitter defeat of the rain gutters. Talk about extremes. Watching in triumph as your shot clears the roof and the neighbor's basketball hoop, only to have that moment brutally cut short when the ball bounces off the roof and comes to a halt with a metallic clang in the gutter.

As soon as the shock and disappointment subsided, hands dove into pockets desperately searching for any spare change that was lurking there among the candy wrappers and baseball cards. Since this was a common occurrence, we knew the magic number. Forty-seven cents, including tax. That is what it took to restore our happiness. Someone was quickly chosen to take the one block run to Casey's using the highly scientific "bubble gum, bubble gum in a dish" method. In moments we had a fresh rubber ball and an assurance that the game would continue, usually well into the night under the friendly glow of the alley's lights.

And still, Casey's was more than a candy-and-rubber-ball supply store. It was the social center of the neighborhood, at least for the under-13 crowd. It was a meeting place, rest stop and dining establishment all in one. If you were looking for someone, you'd look at Casey's; if you wanted to meet somewhere, you'd meet at Casey's; if you wanted to grab a bite to eat before going home to meatloaf night, you'd eat at Casey's.

It was a place in the city where kids could go and be called by name when they walked in the door. We knew Violet and Casey, and they knew us. They knew what grade we were in; they knew our families. We saw them not only in the store, but also in church, walking the dog, going to school, and no matter where it was, there was always a smile and an inquiry as to how we were doing.

Like many of the kids in the neighborhood, I was an altar boy in school. Even though that meant getting up for 6:45 mass once in a while, it had its perks. As morbid as it may sound, one of those perks was serving at funerals. This was a task saved for the older, experienced acolytes. I call this a perk because it meant you got to get out of class for a couple of hours, and were occasionally invited to breakfast. Needless to say, when the priest came into the room asking for volunteers, a shortage is one thing he never had to worry about.

Out of all the funerals that I served for, there is only one that I remember. As we made our way down to church, we engaged in the usual talk—after-school plans, sports, friends. We would then wait in the back of the church for the casket to be brought up and the family to make their way in. Even though we didn't know the people, this moment was always awkward. We had just come from our light-hearted boyhood conversation, and now faced the ultimate pain. We tried not to look at the faces of the people as they filed in. However, this time was different. One face in line we all recognized instantly. This face belonged to Violet. Gone was her smile, her bright expression, her kind voice. Naturally, we frantically scanned the line for another familiar face. We were obviously too young to fully grasp the stinging irony of the situation back then. This man had given us a stoop to rest on and a place to be happy for years. Now, in a sense, we were helping to return the favor.

A majority of my childhood was spent within a three-block area of the city. But in those three blocks, I picked up a world of experience. Even though I have moved since then, I am still within three miles of the neighborhood and return frequently. Casey's is gone, but not forgotten. The large, welcoming store windows are now covered, but the stoop is still there. Kids are still playing dodge ball across the street. And best of all, Violet is also there. I still see her outside walking her dog and, of course, there is still a smile and a warm hello.

Joe Gozdowiak is an English high school teacher in Milwaukee. This is his first published piece.

katherine esposito

In *The Glass Menagerie*, Blanche DeBois depended on the kindness of strangers. But in the city, we get by with a little help from our friends. And the best friends, it turns out, are the ones right next door. I was casting about, halfway to desperate, late for an engagement, wishing for help. My old van had joined the ranks of the dead not an hour before, and although I had a fresh car battery, I'd never put one in. Help arrived in the form of Steve, our babysitter's dad, walking Bess the beagle around the block. "Oh, Steve," I tried not to audibly gasp, "do you know how to install a new car battery?" I knew I really could do it, if it came to that. But if Steve had the necessary know-how and friendly generosity, we might not be as late as I had feared.

"Well, it's been a while since I've done that…." was all he said, as he hustled Bess down the block to fetch a small satchel of tools. Half an hour later, after wrestling with a rusty connection and ill-fitting wrenches, he instructed me to flip on the van's overhead light. It lit. And the kids and I got where we needed to be, a mere 30 minutes late.

I never questioned whether Steve would be gracious enough to help. All I ever privately wondered was whether he knew more about replacing car batteries than I did. Six years spent on the same urban block earns one the privilege to depend on a neighbor in time of need. And they're there, surely, when you least expect and most hope.

The countryside may have more fields and fewer rules, but I think there are distinct advantages to the urban lifestyle. People in my neighborhood sit on stoops and chat through screens and just mosey along, drinking in sounds and smells and flavors in a way that's impossible when traveling 60 on rural roads.

Opportunities for intimacy can manifest unexpectedly. Such as when the 16-year-old across the street experimented with a BB gun one day and accidentally put a hole through our kitchen window. That little incident led to a mom-to-mom discussion of his mourning his dad, which veered into a conversation about my mother, which concluded with a talk about the burdens of single parents, all of which never would have taken place if we hadn't been within waving distance of each other.

Child-rearing tips are proffered, building techniques compared, and lawn care advice tendered over rusty backyard fences, all due to sheer proximity. I never would have guessed that grass would re-sprout so vigorously after being smothered by a children's play tent for two weeks, if I hadn't witnessed such a miracle on my neighbor's lawn. Twice a year I long for air conditioning; this summer it was a relative newcomer two doors down who saved me from insanity, when temperatures had stagnated at 95 degrees-plus and my kids had already seen me slam a cranky telephone on the kitchen floor. Twice a year I wish for a snow blower. Five years ago, I literally ached for one—a neighbor clearing his drive six houses up agreed to do mine in exchange for brownies and cakes.

Step by step, bonds are forged. Over time, I began to feel less like an ostracized divorcee and more like an essential thread in a complex tapestry of community life. I'm the lady in the blue house on the corner. With two boys, a great garden and even better dog, Carmen—a half-shepherd who minds the curb and sidles her way into the hearts of fearful 2- and 3-year-olds.

I'm not sure if a 10-square-mile town can claim such qualities. Villages and rural homesteads are visually lovely but they can invite suspicion, stemming from what neighbors don't know or refuse to understand. On a single city block, secrets are hard to keep, which keeps those backyard fences from rising too tall.

There was a time when I rued this propinquity, when it seemed that my house walls were made of tissue paper and situated just an inch from the next door neighbor's. That was around the time Tim left, after a year of occasional hurled pizza slices and overloud twilight arguments. It was hard to hide that fracas, and I was sure that our all-too-obvious disarray and tortured conversations were heard by all. For a while, I tried hard to turn myself inside-out every time I walked out the door. But the spirit of city life goes well beyond just helping each other. It also includes lapses in memory. Maybe that's because there are just so many of us, all with problems of our own and laundry hanging on the line. Mine happens to include an oversized union suit and 14 pair of boys' briefs.

Steve, my sweetheart of a car-battery-changer, isn't much older than I am, but he's already a grandfather. He lives with his wife, two daughters, a 2-year-old and the beagle, Bess, about seven houses down. Not long ago the neighborhood talk was of his impending patriarchal status. His eldest daughter had gotten herself in a family way just after hitting her 20's, and moved back home.

A baby girl was born and her skin was pretty dark. That was even more of a conversation-starter. But in a relaxed neighborhood like mine, people soon find something else to talk about. Besides, the little girl was awfully cute, with chocolate brown ringlets and a bright smile, and it wasn't all that long before she took to putting a leash on Bess and trundling around the block with her proud grandpa beside her. It was about that time that I heard Steve say that despite living like sardines in their little box of a city house, he didn't really want that half of his family to move out.

I'm sure the rest of my neighbors would agree. Steve's little family is just as perfectly flawed and blissfully happy as any of ours. And just as essential to the fabric—tangled, colorful, and complicated—as is mine.

Katherine Esposito freelances out of a blue house on the corner of a very friendly block in Madison.

zane williams victorian vernacular porch, broom street, madison

a sense of place
Reprinted from Milwaukee Magazine, 1997

kurt chandler

At 8 a.m. on any weekday, the corner of 68th and Lloyd is a whirlpool of stop-and-go activity. Moms and dads fall into rank as they march their children to school. Compulsive morning joggers crisscross paths. Cars and trucks stop and stammer, then bolt through the intersection, the daily chore of getting to work etched across the faces of the drivers.

An hour later, the corner is a portrait of repose. A banner on a HOME FOR SALE sign flutters in the breeze. The crossing guard surrenders her post. A dog owner pauses tentatively as his pet gives the fire hydrant a good sniff.

I pass this corner every morning as I walk my daughter to kindergarten. It's an intersection like most others, an overworked junction that leads to the nearest hardware store, supermarket, freeway ramp and playground. Flashing red lights atop four-way stop signs manage the traffic. Towering oaks shade two-story houses. A white newspaper box dispenses the latest version of crisis and controversy and a familiar blue box collects the mail.

There's no commerce here, no public meeting place, no park bench vista from the shore of a lake or the bank of a river, no real reason to be here at all, other than to pass by.

But as a well-traveled cross point in the grid of avenues and alleys, the intersection serves as a gateway into my community, presenting evidence of the cycles and trends that we follow or ignore.

There are hundreds of these gateways in the city—none of them the same, yet all of them allied in a reflection of community. Impaired by our tunnel-visioned routines, rarely do we notice them. But if we pause and pay attention on our come-and-go routes, these crossroads can provide traces of our identity, hints of who we are and how we live.

On my daily walks, 68th and Lloyd becomes a municipal touchstone. A lawn sign registers political persuasion. A moving sale signals transition. Brightly colored flags hanging from a corner house mark the seasons: Halloween orange, Green Bay green and gold, Easter Egg yellow and purple. And the multi-shades of skin of the children on the sidewalk indicate a growing diversity.

When our daughter was younger and we were new to the neighborhood, she came to recognize this corner every time she saw the flashing red stoplights. "We're almost home," she would say as we walked or drove by. And in her tone was an expression of familiarity, of comfort.

Each time I pass, I share that sense of place.

Kurt Chandler is a senior editor of *Milwaukee Magazine* and author of the book, *Shaving Lessons: A Memoir of Father and Son*.

city lawns

dave cieslewicz

Images flow from the gentle "thrrrrrelk" sound of a reel lawn mower cutting through a small front yard. The scent of fresh cut grass rides on a warm breeze rolling through lace curtains. It mixes with the smell of a hundred ham dinners and apple pies baked into the woodwork of an old house and given up to the breeze only on hot dry summer mornings. It blends with the smell of dusty heat in the attic where you go to find the flag, mid morning on the Fourth of July. It descends to the basement where it joins the bitter sweetness of Eight Brothers tobacco cut by the soapy clean fragrance of Spic 'n Span near the wash tubs.

My grandparents owned a very old reel lawn mower. Once a week I would ride my bike the three miles over cracking city streets from my parents' house in West Allis to my grandparents' bungalow on the South Side of Milwaukee for lawn mowing detail. Starting in May, I would time the weekly cuttings so that I would be sure to make the first July ride on the Fourth.

I liked the feel of the empty streets on the Fourth of July, the heart-breaking beauty and sweet loneliness of a quiet city on the brink of decline. In those days the factory jobs were still good, the unions still strong. On the Fourth of July, I rode down Mitchell Street past huge silent factories, their gates closed, the gatehouses empty. Everyone had left, some of the factory workers to small cottages on lakes "Up North." I imagined them trolling for muskies with puttering Evinrudes beneath perfect blue skies. Or I found them sipping Hamm's on tap in cool, dark, knotty pine supper clubs, waiting for their perch fish fries, talking about the Packers, their conversation punctuated by the clack of billiard balls on tables in the next room.

On that afternoon I had the city to myself. The citizens had left to prettier places, but I loved the narrow alleys, the towering smokestacks and the empty streets they left behind. It was a city that had earned a good rest and it waited contently for its people to return and start the big engine once again.

When I arrived at my grandparents' house on 31st Street, I was greeted with ice-cold lemonade and the invitation to "come sit for awhile before you get started." So I would join them on their porch to hear stories of Fourths past and to talk about what we would do later that day when my father would come to pick us up for the ritual family party in the suburbs. Then I would go to the dilapidated garage, which never housed a car but which was kept immaculate and orderly, to retrieve the heavy iron and wood reel lawn mower. I cut the small yard while my grandmother used the "edger" to clear a narrow channel between the city sidewalk and her lawn, and a weed tool to pry out dandelions.

Edging is mostly a lost art, but like the use of a reel lawn mower, edging is an act of great civility. It is polite. It pays respect to neighbors. Edging says, "I am going to take good care of this 25 feet or so of sidewalk which my city has entrusted to me." The reel lawn mower says, "I am not going to burden you with the roar of an internal combustion engine and I am not going to pollute the air you breathe with its smoke. Instead, I'll provide rhythm for the day's neighborhood music." It mixes well with the cadence of a baseball game on the radio or the smack of a ball into a glove during a game of catch in the street. Thrrrrelk. Rest. Thrrrrelk. Rest. Thrrrrelk.

This kind of civility is possible only where the lawns are small. Big lawns demand grotesque techniques of husbandry. Vast lagoons of grass must be routed with thirteen-horsepower engines. Weeding by hand would be a lost cause too. Chemical warfare is the only thing that works. And edging? Well, edging requires an edge.

A small yard and a common sidewalk to take care of allow for civility; they cultivate politeness and a gentle urban decency. The large lawn makes demands for air wars and ground troops to keep it in check and thereby keep up appearances for the lawn's own sake. A small yard connects a person to his neighbors. A sidewalk connects a citizen to his city. Big yards and no sidewalks say that we're going it alone.

These days, when I cut the grass at my own old house in my own old neighborhood in a different Wisconsin city, I remember those lawn-cutting excursions to my grandparents. My reel lawn mower cuts a "thrrrrelk" sound as I push it through my small yard. I greet neighbors on the sidewalk as they pause, inviting conversation and giving me a break from the job. When they move on down the street, I think of conversations with my grandmother as we manicured her lawn with tools of quiet urban dignity late mornings on the Fourth of July. On my porch a glass of lemonade sweats in the midday heat and waits for me to pick it up.

Dave Cieslewicz is the director of 1000 Friends of Wisconsin, Inc. He and his wife, Dianne, and their dog, Fern, live in one of Madison's old neighborhoods, where you can find him on summer weekends cutting his lawn the old-fashioned way.

sunday morning

Nobody goes to church much anymore,
though no one does much of anything else
so it's quiet, or as quiet as it gets;

usually there's a saw or somebody's mower,
a drill or a hammer hating another
repair we will have to live with

and the rare home run from the ballpark
and the pulse and trailing whisper
of the sprinklers when it's dry

and old deaf Winslow's blind
old cocker spaniel winds itself up
short around the clothes pole again

and the soft—almost apologetic—
screen door's screech and slam,
the trash can's guilty clatter after dark.

Bruce Taylor is currently a professor of English at the University of Wisconsin-Eau Claire. His poetry has appeared in numerous publications, including *The Chicago Review, the Formalist, Gulf Coast, The Literary Review, The Nation, The New York Quarterly, Poetry* and his most recently published book, *This Day*, published by Juniper Press. He has won awards and fellowships from the Wisconsin Arts Board, the National Endowment for the Arts, and the Bush Arts Foundation.

neighbors

rachel nuetzel, rufus king high school

My house is located on 88th and Grantosa. A small neighborhood stretched out over long city blocks. Close to a nearby middle school with adequate access to the Milwaukee County Transit System and local stores. Our house is smack in the middle of a block with a fire hydrant and a school crossing sign in front.

Our houses are not parted by a lot of space. From my bedroom window, I can see into my neighbor's kitchen. The back door pretty much lines up with my window, and at night their track light shines brilliantly into my room. The light is sometimes an annoyance and keeps me up, but other times I just ignore it.

I hear the two neighbor brothers yelling and slamming the side door. I look at the clock and it reads 2 a.m. One of the brothers has locked the other out of the house and will not let him in. The following morning, I can smell food being cooked on a grill. This is not weird—the neighbor men grill out every day. I do not think they know how to use the stove.

My cat is tied up outside on her leash and the neighbor dog, Jessie, comes over to play. One of the neighbors yells for Jessie to return, but she does not because our dog, Thunder, has joined her outside. The two dogs chase each other and nip at each other's necks. They run up and down the sidewalk, until finally both are retrieved. Once again, it is nightfall and I smell chicken cooking on the grill.

Tonight starts with silence, although I can hear the wind against my window. I can hear the shouts of young adults down the road as they gather in front of their apartments talking and drinking. The track light is turned on. I can make finger puppets on my walls. The wind cracks again. I can now hear an ambulance and police cars racing down our street.

I often sit on the porch and watch. I can hear the neighbors talking, but no conversation takes place with me. They live so close, but seem so far away. But I cannot complain. They are part of this safe neighborhood and help maintain that comfort. When I lock myself out of the house and cannot manage to get in through the window, my neighbors are there. All I just have to do is ring their doorbell and I am invited to stay. When there is not enough milk, sugar or eggs, I can go over and ask if they have any. Most of the time they do! They may not know my name, but that doesn't seem to matter.

We live so close, but don't socialize regularly. They may keep me up at night with their hollering and slamming of doors, and may wake me up early by mowing the lawn or grilling out, but that is all right. Neighbors are the ones who build a community, good or bad. So as I sit in my room or on the front step, I feel safe. The community in which I live gives me comfort. We have social neighbors, and I hope the members of my family are also viewed as social, acceptable neighbors. I like to hear the voices of the adults, kids playing, stereo systems wailing, cars racing by, the slamming of doors, and people yelling.

All of these things bring comfort and add to life and experience. Neighbors are a very important part of how one lives. They may seem annoying, but just remember, it could also be worse.

Rachel Nuetzel attended Rufus King High School in Milwaukee and currently studies pre-vet and wildlife management at the University of Minnesota.

veronica bieganski, rufus king high school

People are often asked about their origins. All I have to say is "This is where I have been raised and no matter where I move, it will always be home." And, if you will, my home is your home. Though, if you can't come for a visit, I will try to give you a taste of a culture that ranges from the most passive to the most unrestrained ever offered in one location. Here, from the four corners of this great city, is Milwaukee!

The cry of the South Side cannot be heard while the sun shines its rays, though as the moon graces us with its beams, the South Side stirs; havoc can be tasted in the air. It is the home of one of the most famous streets in Milwaukee, Mitchell Street. If you are as game as I am, you will be interested in what the summer has to offer you here. You are invited into every store that is open, greeted by all the amazing street vendors, and asked to partake in the festivals that are being held. Life on the South Side is created by the atmosphere that began long before your time. It began with the immigration of the Polish, followed by the Mexican. The South Side is still predominantly made up of the Mexican and the Polish. Though it is also home to many other groups, and the rich environment of one of the nation's leading women's colleges, Alverno College.

The West Side, it can be said, is reserved for some rich but not extravagant people. To go along with the bounty, there are parks that are managed by some of the most caring people in the world. There are large golf courses, flowerbeds, play structures and more than enough baseball, football and soccer fields. I am not saying that this is the only place where these can be found; but let's just say a lot of them can be found in this neck of the woods.

The north sides of cities are thought to be troublesome in all parts of the world, no matter where you are. Well, it is no different here, with the exception that we know how to hide it better. The news that is brought into our homes from this neighborhood every day is like no other. We have the crime, the poor, the problems, and everything that goes along with being a major city. It has been heard from great sources in the area that life on the North Side is as unpredictable as the weather in Wisconsin. People have learned to watch out for one another, to care for one another deeply, because no matter who you think you are, you are never safe from what goes bump in the night.

Then finally, there is the East Side. It does not matter who you are, what you do, your age, or what you want to accomplish with your life. The East Side has welcomed all types, and has become the adoptive home for so many, including myself. I always know that I can return there, no matter what goes on. However, the only thing that does matter here is that you keep an open mind to what you will see, and what will see you. Some of the best concerts, clubs and art displays are here, all open for the wondering and questioning mind.

The way a life is lived is not really determined by government officials here, but it is dictated by how open your mind is to change. The more open you are to experiences, the more fun you will have while you visit our city. If you ever wanted to experience what the essence of existence is, Milwaukee is the place to see how far you can go. Though, before you dive in without looking, please remember this: You are always welcome, but start off in the shallow end first…

Veronica Bieganski is currently a student at University of Wisconsin—Stevens Point studying accounting and special education. She looks forward to writing more in her future.

mary jo walicki children playing at 22nd and north

a sense of community

brent nicastro downtown biker

the blue plate special

eve tai

In the summer of 1990, I arrived home in Madison after living in Paris for a year. Though I didn't have a job yet, I was secure knowing that I had just tasted some of life's pleasures, and felt confident that good things lay ahead. Little did I know that some of those would be found at a place called Monty's Blue Plate Diner.

The diner was a new restaurant in the neighborhood. When I had left town, it was a place of concrete and weeds. The owner and his business partners had re-habbed an old gas station into a sleek diner featuring very good comfort food. In fact, the owner's parents had met on the very sidewalk in front of the old gas station years ago. The story intrigued me, and I decided to wait tables there while I looked for a more permanent job.

I didn't really know much about waitressing, but fortunately, my lack of experience was lost in the chaos of the restaurant's opening weeks, when the Blue Plate was still trying to figure out its systems. Arguments erupted between the waitstaff and the cooks, the busboys wanted a higher cut from the waitstaff tips, the espresso machine was delicate and fussy. I found these workplace issues kind of novel and as a result, could maintain an easy distance. I was more focused on meeting and observing all the interesting customers who were coming in the doors.

Flooding in was more like it. It soon became apparent that the Blue Plate's appeal stretched far beyond our immediate neighborhood, and included folks from literally next door to hundreds of miles away in Minneapolis. The crowds almost never slowed down, no matter the time of day or day of the week. The customers all shared a good appetite, of course, but their appetite wasn't just for food. There was a liveliness about them, an eagerness to be there. Even folks from Chicago, their faces worn from years of long commutes and working in sealed high-rises, would just blossom when they walked in the door. One day, as I waited on two booths that were sharing a conversation between them about the latest city council meeting, it dawned on me. Our customers were also hungry for community.

At the time, Madison had a decent culinary scene, so there were plenty of places to get a good meal. But not many restaurants offered the sense of neighborhood that the Blue Plate did, nor could they match its homey, yet arty decor of appliance sculptures swirling with glowing neon tubes. I had worked during my summers off from college at a suburban country club in Detroit, and was accustomed to a fair degree of surliness from the members. But at the Blue Plate, folks smiled while giving their orders for the "Meatloaf of the Gods" (a favorite) and a microbrew, and frequently seemed happy to chat with me.

The variety of people who came to the Blue Plate reminded me of something a friend of mine used to say— "same planet, different worlds." I couldn't imagine where else you would find all these folks sitting next to each other as though they were in their own kitchens. In one month's time, I waited on a graphic designer, a famous musician, a crusty farmer, lesbian couples, the local warm-and-fuzzy weather guy from Channel 15, a poet living in New York back to see his hometown, a little boy who ordered his Oreo shake in sign language, a police officer, lady golfers sporting diamond golf club pins and even an old boss visiting from Chicago with his grandchildren.

To appreciate the mix of people who came to the Blue Plate, it helps to know a little bit about Madison culture.

Monty's is on the East Side of Madison, a part of town with an industrial blue-collar history. Cozy neighborhoods with bungalows weave their way around Lake Monona, taking in local shops that sometimes haven't been remodeled for 25 years or more and probably won't be for another 25. In the 1960s, the East Side was also a hippy haven, with head shops and funky souls strewn along Williamson Street, better known as Willy Street. A faint haze still hangs around the area, and residents are often proud of their counterculture history, even as the old men in thick glasses still take in the sun in front of the old-fashioned Ace Hardware store.

As the city's population grew, so did the city's boundary. Residents spread west in search of more space and larger homes, bringing with them more roads and strip malls. The migration mimicked trends found in larger cities across the nation in the '60s and '70s, only instead of "white flight," it was more like "white-collar flight." Over time, West Siders were reluctant to go "all the way over" to the East Side, when so many of life's conveniences were only a car ride away.

So when Monty's Blue Plate started drawing in crowds from the West Side, that was something remarkable. Even as crowds bulged the diner's doors on weekend brunch days, no one seemed to mind the chaos or their hunger, which would only sharpen to a delicious level with the wait. The wait also gave you a chance to ease into the day with a cup of fresh coffee and some socializing—you almost always bumped into someone you knew, or at least wanted to know. At the Blue Plate, you helped create the atmosphere merely by being there.

After a few months, I found a job and went back to the 9-to-5 life. But I continued to return to the Blue Plate almost as often as when I had worked there. I thought that over time I would grow bored of going to Monty's. But nearly 10 years rolled by, and that never happened. The place was irresistible. I loved everything about it. I joined friends for breakfast there so often that we didn't have to specify where to meet when we made plans. I went to the Blue Plate when I was feeling lonely, maybe with a book or a letter to write, or to read the New York Times, soaking up the hum of human energy around me. I walked out on a beau once in the middle of my grain burger, and had lively meetings with colleagues, no doubt fueling our creativity with Monty's breakfast biscuits loaded with honey and butter.

We live in a time when many of our creative powers are devoted to making us more independent. Cars, automated teller machines, and most notably computer technology have made our lives easier and more convenient. But if we are to believe that these things which make us independent also remove our need for each other, then we are believing an illusion. We still need to connect with each other, to feel a part of something bigger. We need to know that there are other people out there, and that we have a place alongside them.

Even as we are prone to point out our differences, we are more often longing for common ground. Community, in the truest sense of the word, is both found and created at Monty's Blue Plate. Maybe not on a huge scale, but a significant one all the same. It isn't a special occasion kind of place. Rather, the Blue Plate is special because it is an everyday kind of place. It has something for everyone—an idea that our supposedly more sophisticated lifestyles have almost forgotten or no longer thought possible. But we know it is. Just walk into the Blue Plate on any day, and our neighbors are there, engaged in the important business of another day in their lives.

Eve Tai lived in Madison for 12 years before an irresistible job offer in Seattle drew her to that special city. She returns often to Madison and her favorite table at the Blue Plate.

finding our way back downtown

jane tappen

My husband and I live in a drafty 100-year-old Victorian house at the north edge of the rim that circles downtown Eau Claire. From our back yard, we look down on the heart of Eau Claire—the church spires that dot the inner city, historic city hall, the brick buildings of downtown, the old Uniroyal tire plant that is now a mixed-used complex called Banbury Place, the confluence of the Eau Claire and Chippewa Rivers, the wooded riverbanks.

Work is just a walk away. In July 1999, I joined my husband in the ranks of those who work downtown. My workday mornings are now spent letting my mind wander while my legs do the work rather than forcing my sleepy head to be alert to traffic hazards while steering through heavy traffic on the way to a job on the fringes. On winter mornings, the time I used to spend warming up my car while I scraped ice from the windshield can now be spent pausing on my walk to watch the steam rising from the Chippewa River.

But my walk has a catch. Although our house is only three blocks from my workplace, the connecting street, Dewey Street, was cut in two by the city in the '80s to carve out a city arterial at the base of the hillside with a railroad bridge overhead. Just one of the city's many "improvements" that accommodated cars and nothing else. To get downtown, you have to walk down stairs to reach the arterial where the sidewalk is right next to speeding traffic that sprays you with gravel in the warm season and slush in the winter. Or you can take the alternate route: go to the end of Dewey Street, climb over a fence, cross the railroad tracks, and then climb over another fence to connect with Dewey on the other side.

Each day, I leave my dignity at home and take my over-the-fence route to work (no skirts or heels allowed). Sometimes I meet other neighbors, including kids, taking the same route. One neighbor said with a smile as we passed on the tracks, "so you found the best way to get downtown too." We make the best of what we have. But meanwhile, we're lobbying the city for a pedestrian bridge that will reconnect our neighborhood to the downtown.

Like many older working-class neighborhoods, the North Side Hill has always been a mixing pot of nationalities. According to a local history account, in the late 1800s the neighborhood was mostly Irish, but by the 1900s you could find the Swedish Johnsons, the Norwegian Johnsons, and the Irish Johnsons all within one block, and the distinction always had to be made when any one talked about the Johnsons. Over the years, the need for that distinction faded away. In the early 1980s new immigrant names arrived—the Xiongs, the Mouas, the Hers, and the Lees. Many of these Hmong families settled into the older neighborhoods of Eau Claire where they found roomy homes at reasonable prices. Today more than 80 Hmong families call the North Side Hill home. New faces, new challenges for finding new ways to come together as a neighborhood while respecting and appreciating our differences.

The homes in our neighborhood are mostly pre-1940 wood-frame, three-bedroom, two-story homes. Average price of a home: $60,000. When we were shopping for homes, this big, old house with its wide oak woodwork, high ceilings, and open staircase seemed like a beauty for the price. When the assessor came through, he said if this was on the "right" side of town, you'd have paid $30,000 more. I told the assessor that we felt confident that we were on the *right* side of town.

Our neighborhood school, Longfellow School, originally built in 1885 with several additions added, is one of the few old two-story brick schools in Eau Claire that has not been replaced by a new one-story sprawling school. We are proud of our well-maintained neighborhood school with its colorful halls, where the majority of the children still walk to school. More than 400 students attend Longfellow; 30 percent of that population is minorities. We're hoping that the school will be successful in its plan to host a weekly family night where a meal is served along with educational and recreational activities for all ages. Such a weekly gathering would be a boom for community-building in our neighborhood, a time set aside to socialize and connect.

Our neighborhood has the foundation to be a livable neighborhood—close to downtown, diverse and affordable, with a neighborhood school and three neighborhood parks—two overlooking Dells Pond, one with a panoramic view of the city. What we need is the building blocks—committed neighbors, concerned elected officials, informed city staff—to refocus our attention from the fringes to our core.

There is much character in the heart of Eau Claire, but the money isn't there. Over most of the past few decades, that's gone to the fringes—the suburbs, the malls, the interstate intersections—leaving the downtown with little foot traffic and struggling businesses. In a few years, I hope to report we have a pedestrian bridge giving us easy access to the downtown where the now empty storefronts will be filled with businesses that draw the neighbors in—businesses like a grocery store, a full-service bookstore, a local cafe. Places where we will have ample opportunity to meet our neighbors in attractive downtown spaces rather than out in the cold on the railroad tracks.

We bucked the migration to the outskirts and chose to invest in this inner-city, working-class neighborhood called the North Side Hill. A neighborhood that some say is on the wrong side of the tracks. A neighborhood that we say is a survivor a bit down on its luck, but with the grit for revival.

Jane Tappen and her husband, Jay, have lived in Eau Claire since 1991. Jane works as a publication coordinator for an architectural firm and devotes much of her spare time to community building through neighborhood organizing. She is currently helping to design a pilot project that would create a formal place for citizen involvement early in the city's street project planning process, a place where citizens can discuss issues, concerns, and ideas with city staff before the street is designed.

tim holte mrs. brandenburg with fluffy

the people you meet

I love my dogs, and it is with not a small portion of pride that I lead them around the city. They are large and handsome—a juvenile black-and-white Newfoundland the size of a small horse, and a shepherd with keen, mournful eyes and a sleek black coat. Strangers stop me in the supermarket to compliment them and, by the simple extension of a light six-foot lead, myself.

I have formed a bond with the woman who works the register at the cafeteria where I work based on our connections with shepherds. Her sister and her kids have a beautiful dog, only 2 years old, with serious health problems. Lately every time I come to buy coffee, she tells me about another medical procedure the dog has undergone. We know how that kind of thing affects the kids, not to mention the adults.

There is a beautiful brown boy named Timothy with bare feet, no shirt, a braid hanging down his back, and a smile like bougainvillea, who all summer has raced through the park across the street from my house to pet the Newfoundland every time we enter. He pronounces the dog's strange Indian name, Aanimush, carefully and with pride, like a famous poem he has memorized. I used to let him hold the lead until the time the other kids ran at the dog, who in turn, attempted to run them down. Aanimush started dragging Timothy across the grass toward the other kids who were tentatively running away, waiting to see if he would hold the dog back or be pulled down. I found myself being short with Timothy even though it wasn't his fault. It was hard for me that day to watch the flower of his smile wilt with the harshness of my words. The next day I made sure the other kids stood back, made sure the dogs knew who was boss, before I gave the lead to Timothy. And they walked politely just behind his heels, the way the dog trainer told me they should walk, like employees, which was a great happiness for him. Sometimes I take the dogs about a mile away down to Turtle Creek Park, their favorite place on this earth, though not as often as they would like because it is such an ordeal to get them there. It means putting them in the car, parking with the motorcycles and pick-ups in the lot of The Watering Hole, then walking back over the bridge to the park. The sidewalk leading to the bridge is located on the other side of the highway, requiring me to run across four lanes of traffic. And since I don't run with them very often, the damn dogs think we are playing. They stop to jump and bite each other while the semis bear down. I'm trying not to imagine them dead, mashed flat, disemboweled, as I yank with all my might on their leads, yelling "With me! With me!" like I learned in dog school. This is why I do not come to Turtle Creek Park very often.

This park is actually little more than a ribbon of asphalt and a narrow plot of patchy grass. On one side is the rippling rush of the creek, edged and overhung with maple, chestnut, and walnut, each at the cusp of whatever fall drama they are to perform. On the other side, through a Cyclone fence and beyond the railroad tracks, are a series of car dealers and an RV lot. I let the dogs go, and they run off to sniff the ancient playground equipment, rusted and squeaking—monumental—in the wind. I cannot read the date etched on the metal plate underneath the jungle gym, but that makes it old enough.

Just beyond the playground is a partially fenced area where a pool used to be. There's a sign on the fence that says NO TRESPASSING. But then a few steps further, the fence abruptly ends, and you can walk right onto the cement walkway that skirted what had been the pool, which is now a rectangle of coarse-bladed grass. This is where the high school girls and boys used to lay out their winter-white backs and bellies and dream about love. Beyond the pool is the old bathhouse. The windows are all boarded up, but the doors open wide into the most extreme darkness, and you can still see the outline of the words, CREEK PARK POOL, across the cornice. Standing in the large rectangle of grass with the cement border, looking up at these faded words, I feel like a squirrel in a graveyard.

Beyond the pool is the softball field. As I enter the infield area with the dogs in the lead, I see (with a little dread, I admit) a man who looks a little like Latrelle Sprewell, the basketball star, with his see-through goatee, braided hair and long, straight nose. I have seen this man around. He is someone who drinks and begs for money, I think. In the past, I have crossed the street to avoid meeting him face to face. One time he called to me from across the street. Nice dogs, he shouted out. Nice dogs you got. The fact is that I do not know that he begs. I only know that he approaches strangers and talks to them until they give him something, and then they scurry away. This I have witnessed perhaps three times. I have also seen him drunk, weaving down the sidewalk on the bridge we just crossed to get into the park. There is no street to cross here. I stand on the pitcher's rubber watching the dogs run the bases, as the man walks deliberately toward me from the left field corner like a relief pitcher coming to replace me.

"You have some nice dogs," he says when he gets within about a 10-foot range. "I've admired them many times." Three steps later he holds his hand out (if I'd had a basketball, I would have given it to him) and I shake it. Does it matter that his grip was unusually weak, like that of someone with a terminal illness?

"My name is Robert," he says. He is wearing a gray pin-stripe sports coat, a button-down blue shirt and khaki slacks—the clothes of a moderately successful man out for a stroll on Saturday. After I consider claiming to a Brett, or Tony, or Jean-Paul, I tell him my name.

"Can I ask you something?" he says, pulling out a folded piece of paper from his jacket pocket. The paper is some kind of human resources form with a couple names and phone numbers written in one corner. "You see that name there? I was supposed to call Bob on Tuesday about starting work, I was going to tell him that he could depend on me, that I was a good worker." I nod with as much feeling as I can. "And then the woman gives me this test, like tell me what numbers you see, and all there is to see is a bunch of dots, there weren't no numbers. She told me I had to go get my eyes checked before I could start the job, and it might be until next Friday, and I don't have enough money, Christ, I haven't had a drink for a week. I thought all I had to do was pee in the cup and that went all right—hadn't had a drink in eight days. I'm a good worker, but I don't have the money for no eye doctor."

Robert seems to have spit this out in less time than it would have taken me to say Jack Frost. And I don't know what he's asking for—compassion, or money for the eye doctor, or nothing at all but someone to tell his story to. He takes his wallet out and gives me an identification card that has his picture on it and his name. Robert. Just like he says. "You see, this is me," he says, pointing to the name on the top of the human resources form. "Things are not going that well for me right now, you know," he says. His posture is sympathetic, somehow, making me want to put my arm around his shoulders to hold him up. "I'm out here." He waves his arm in a way to take in the baseball diamond and everything else.

We stand for a minute without talking and watch the dogs chase each other around the bases. "I had a dog once. Loved that dog," he says. "Then it went and bit someone and I had to put it down. That about killed me."

"Same thing happened to me," I answer, and a tear forms in the corner of my eye as I think of my old friend, Basho, who bit the child who lives next door.

"It's a funny thing about how you get attached to a dog," Robert says, and he tries to lure Aanimush over to him by making little kissing sounds with his lips. But the dog will not come close. Then he fishes in his pocket and brings out an old peanut butter cracker—the bright orange kind you can get in gas station machines—and holds it out toward the dogs that then come to him in a gallop. He breaks the cracker in half and gives a part to each dog. They swallow without chewing, and look at him for more.

"That's all I have. Sorry," he tells them, but they won't leave him. I notice that I, too, have moved closer, am standing almost hip to hip with Robert, like we're old friends thinking back to something we each would have forgotten forever if we had not happened to meet.

Bill New teaches about children and education at Beloit College, near which he lives with his spouse, their two children, Xeno and Yuma, and their two dogs. He is currently working on a project concerning reform schools and the Chicago juvenile court at the end of the 19th century.

the gathering
Reprinted from Milwaukee Magazine, 1999

marie kohler

There is no night more sweet or full of promise than a Friday in Milwaukee.

The work week is over, the weekend not yet begun—we are like kids sprung from the last day of school. Across the city in taverns, church halls and restaurants we gather, lines forming where the air is thick with the scent of battered fish meeting hot oil.

We sit, peruse the crowd, have a golden lager and absorb the heady buzz of friends and families, talking, laughing, waiting. Then it comes, golden, piled high on plates with bowls of french fries, mounds of slaw and marbled rye. We eat, forks and fingers revealing the white, delicate steaming flakes. We drink, the beer swilling inside our mouths, putting out the fire with perfect chemistry.

Consider our rare good fortune: Except for rumors of scattered fish fries in other nearby states, there are few Friday fish fries as we know them outside of Wisconsin. Why, we wonder, are we so fortunate?

The custom's origins are stubbornly mysterious. It all starts, of course, with the Catholic Church's tradition of meatless Fridays, an ancient reference to the day of Jesus' death. But there are many areas around the country just as Catholic with nothing like our Friday fish fries—not in Boston, not in New York. Nah, it's a German custom, locals crow—the beer, the gemütlichkeit! But nearly half of our German immigrants were Lutheran, and Germans in Ohio or Pennsylvania know no such sweet delights.

Some say the custom arose after Prohibition, when taverns offered something extra to draw families to the bars. Others trace it back to the rowdy French Canadian trappers of the 1700s who turned to fishing as the fur trade started to collapse.

Milwaukee's Friday night fish fry may best be seen as a happy accident of history, a providential blending of cultures through time and proximity to Lake Michigan and its once abundant perch.

But perhaps it is that historic link to church, to community that gives this decidedly local event its distinctive good-vibe feel. A gathering of like-minded people feeding their flock while fueling their causes—as with Serb Hall's St. Sava Cathedral volunteers or the free-thinking tumblers at old Turner Hall.

The truth is, fish fries are both secular and sacred, our ritual celebration in the company of those who prize tradition and food as we do. A shared experience that says: It's Friday in Milwaukee and we're blessed.

Wisconsin born and bred, Marie Kohler is a freelance writer, actor, theater producer and playwright. A graduate of Harvard and UWM and the mother of two, she is happy to make Milwaukee her home.

john roach

We all like to think we are unique.

We might do something odd to our hair. Wear red shoes. Drive a Humvee. Just a little something to set ourselves apart from the herd. Me, I wear a bow tie occasionally. Dorky, I know. But hey, I tie it myself.

But now I have no need for that affectation. Why? Well, lo and behold, I have found that I'm already unique. And I became so by doing absolutely nothing. My claim to singularity? You are not going to believe this, but I was actually born and raised in Madison, Wisconsin!

Yup—entered this earth at St. Mary's Hospital. Kindergartened at Randall Grade School under the firm but loving hand of the Dominican nuns. Had the legendary Earl Wilke for gym class at Edgewood High School. Even went to the UW and got myself tear-gassed.

I am a walking, talking rarity in area code 608. I am a townie. My guess is that there are three of us left: me, Pat Richter and Henry Busch. If you don't know who Henry Busch is—well, you're no townie.

With our burg growing in national acclaim for its livability, more folks have made their way here to our shores. Add those new folks to the tens of thousands who came to the U and never left, transferred in with Oscar Mayer, or just pulled off the interstate to use a restroom, and the percentage of Madisonians who were actually born and raised in the "City by the Lakes" is reaching extinct proportions. You would be amazed at the Madisonians who aren't from Madison. Mayor Sue Bauman? New York. Police Chief Williams? Tennessee. Fire Chief Amesqua? Minnesota. School Superintendent Rainwater? Arkansas.

No wonder these folks have had a hard time getting anything done. They don't know anyone! Tammy Baldwin is the only Madison politician who is actually from here, and she just moved away to Washington.

Now don't get me wrong. We townies are not ones to be cool to visitors, even if they are the mayor of the town they are visiting. In fact, we want all these foreigners to fit in. So here's the plan. I am going to teach you tourists to talk townie. Create some instant Madison memories for you. Then the next time you're in a conversation with a real Madisonian, you can drop one of these morsels and boom! You're as Madison as Manchester's. (Note: Manchester's was a department store on the Square. The Square was a place Madisonians used to shop.)

Two important points before the lesson begins. First, Madison is really two towns separated by a common isthmus—the East Side and the West Side. The East Side is blue-collar—Gisholt and Oscar Mayer country. The West Side is Whitecollarville comprised of 500 UW professors and the guys at Oscar Mayer who manage the Oscar Mayer guys who live on the East Side.

By the way, Maple Bluff is an anomaly. Millions of years ago, aliens visited Earth. Through some strange technology having to do with ions, they were able to move an entire section of Lake Forest, Illinois, and drop it on the shores of Lake Mendota. I saw a documentary about this recently on the Discovery Channel.

The second thing you need to know is that Madison history can be divided into two eras, BS and AS: Before Soglin and After Soglin. The arrival of Paul (from Chicago, by the way) and a whole generation of anti-war activists, hippies and Black Panthers changed Madison's reputation. It gave us one. Before Soglin we were just another college town. After Soglin we were interesting.

A couple of townies, Karl Armstrong and his little brother Dwight actually made us more interesting than we cared to be.

Anyhow, sit up class. Here's how to talk Madison. Repeat after me:

"Yeah, but he's no Joe Franklin." Joe was one of the finest basketball players to ever wear the Badger red and white. And one of the school's first African American athletes. He played in the early '60s. Joe graduated from the old Central High, which is now a vocational school. You get extra credit if you throw in the name of his coach, Boomer Harris, another Madison legend.

"Yum! This must have been cooked in The Bush." Say this any time you have good Italian food. The Bush (short for "Greenbush") was Madison's old Italian neighborhood, near where St. Joe's Parish used to be, which is where there's something now that no one will ever talk about wistfully.

"Monkeys? Let me tell you about monkeys!" When the talk turns to primates, start musing about the day the monkeys got away at Vilas Zoo. Some keeper left a gate open and the critters took off into the Arboretum like apes. I think they're still finding them in there. Extra credit in zoo history if you mention your memories of the Fourth of July fireworks at Vilas or the Winkey the Elephant tragedy.

When someone mentions that they saw the singer from Garbage at the Café Montmartre, pipe up and say, "Yeah, well I saw JFK on the Square and Arnie Palmer at Odana."

JFK did a campaign whip around the Square in the fall of 1959 in the late Vince Sweeney's blue Lincoln Continental. Arnie blew into town and played Odana when it was new. He launched a drive that rolled to rest many yards out on the 16th fairway. There is now a boulder there to mark the spot. They call it "Arnie's Rock."

"Yeah, but he's not Dave Raven in the bird cage." With all respect to Johnny, Sly, and the other hard-working jocks in town, there was a time when WISM-AM ruled the world. Madison's first rock station featured Jay O' Day, Clyde Coffee and Dave Raven. In our version of the time the turkeys were thrown from the plane on WKRO, WISM once did a promotion in which they buried a certificate redeemable for several thousand dollars inside a lipstick container (called a "golden capsule"), and then issued cryptic clues as to its whereabouts. Folks went around with flashlights and shovels and tore the city apart. A young girl eventually found the treasure in the "Lost City." Extra points if you can locate the Lost City. Even more points if you can respond to the Dave Raven line with "Yeah, but he was no Jim Mader."

Someone is talking to you online and you tap out "I'd rather be making a gimp lanyard." During the summers of the '50s and '60s the city created a park program that kept kids busy all around town, from Wingra to Tenny. Teenagers would be hired to work with younger kids and teach them all the things a well-respecting Madison child should know: how to play washers, tether ball, mill and most important, how to weave stuff for your parents made out of gimp, a plastic yarn that came in wonderfully vivid colors. All of the makings of a wonderful summer were kept in small, mysterious sheds at each park. The parks were also alive with flyweight and midget baseball games, and a strange activity that used to take place in our lakes. We called it "swimming."

So there is your lesson, complete. Just bark out Joe Franklin's or Dave Raven's name. Invoke The Bush or gimp. And presto, you're a townie!

And then you will find—unlike in the rest of the world, which boasts the famous Six Degrees of Separation—that you're a member of a community in which the law of Two Degrees rules. In Madison, if you're a townie, you're only one person away from knowing a friend or acquaintance.

And in a time when our society has become more transient and rootless, that makes us, well, unique. Just ask Henry Busch.

John Roach is president of John Roach Projects, an Emmy award-winning video and film production company, specializing in broadcast, corporate communication and commercial production. John co-wrote the screenplay for "The Straight Story," a film directed by David Lynch. The film's star, Richard Farnsworth, received an Academy Award nomination for Best Actor.

new urbanism comes to wisconsin

Adapted from material originally published in the Milwaukee Journal Sentinel on June 1, 1999.

whitney gould

When was it that the American Dream of a big house on a big lot in the suburbs started to curdle? Was it when the commute from home to work turned into a headache? Or when mowing that yawning expanse of bluegrass began to eat up much of a weekend? Or when people realized that they didn't know their neighbors?

Out of just such discontent over the isolation and frustrations of suburban life was born New Urbanism, a land-use reform movement that seeks to re-create the density, diversity and pedestrian orientation of traditional neighborhoods.

It's a movement that's finding fertile ground in Wisconsin.

Instead of rigidly separated zoning, with houses, shops and workplaces miles from each other, New Urbanism mixes things up a bit. Smaller houses on modest lots, with apartments and condos mixed in, all within walking distance of stores, parks and other public spaces. A daily commute as easy on foot or by mass transit as by car. Buildings built close to the street, which are made more narrow.

The results: slower traffic, less dependence on the automobile, less waste of land and more neighborliness. Well, that's the theory. The reality is that scattered, auto-dependent development is still the dominant land-use pattern nationwide.

"Sprawl will be with us for at least another decade," says Milwaukee Mayor John O. Norquist, a founder of the Congress for New Urbanism. "But the market has begun to discover that New Urbanism is a respectable choice. It's all about getting more value out of real estate by rediscovering some time-tested rules of planning."

There are about 400 New Urbanist communities being developed nationwide. About half are in suburban areas; the rest are "infill" developments, built on vacant or underused tracts within cities.

Middleton Hills, a newer subdivision west of Madison, is Wisconsin's first suburban example. CityHomes, developed in Milwaukee's Midtown Triangle neighborhood, typifies the infill approach.

Milwaukee, in fact, has become a hotbed of New Urbanism. A proposed master plan for the downtown is a virtual textbook of compact, walkable development; guidelines for new development citywide are based on the same principles. The approach is shaping several new neighborhoods, from Cherokee Point on the southwest side to East Pointe and its spinoffs on the lower east side. Hillside Terrace, a troubled public housing project on the near north side, was reconstructed to national acclaim along New Urbanist lines, with through-streets, porch-enhanced townhouses and other pedestrian amenities.

Outside Milwaukee, the movement has been slower to catch on, thanks in part to local zoning regulations that mandate big houses on big lots and prohibit mixed uses. But that may be starting to change. Jackson, in Washington County, is sprouting a New Urbanist subdivision. Elements of New Urbanism are turning up in planning and redevelopment efforts under way in New Berlin, Brookfield, Hales Corners, Franklin, Germantown, Racine, Kenosha and Madison.

For 18 years, Ron and Barb Perkins lived in a conventional subdivision in Madison. Big yards. Big houses set far back from the street. They knew only a handful of their neighbors. Now, as residents of Middleton Hills, a 150-acre community being carved out of a rolling, wooded site just west of Madison, the Perkinses know just about everybody in sight—including a woman from their old neighborhood whom they had never met in all the years the two families lived near each other. In the alley behind the Perkinses' house—yes, the alley—there are summer picnics. Neighbors, who live cheek-by-jowl and close to the street, meet and greet on the sidewalk, wave from their porches or chat at the communal mail drop.

Closeness. Alleys. Sidewalks. Front porches. Smaller houses on small lots on narrow streets. This is the face of New Urbanism, the planning philosophy on which Middleton Hills is built. The movement is in many ways a new twist on the Old Urbanism: the kind of dense, walkable development that defined American communities before World War II and the explosion of sprawling, auto-dependent suburbs.

Reality check: With only 40 houses built so far, retail at Middleton Hills for now is limited to a small convenience store subsidized by the developer; residents here and in many New Urbanist subdivisions remain dependent on their cars. "But if we have enough of these communities nationwide, we'll have less reliance on the automobile," says Paul Brunsell, project director for Middleton Hills, which was launched in 1993 by Marshall Erdman & Associates.

Residents like the Perkinses, with two grown sons, have bought into this close-knit lifestyle without regrets. "There's a sense of bonding in a place like this," says Barb. "It's wonderful being part of a real neighborhood," says Ron, 53, who runs an insurance agency out of the ground floor of their cozy home—something that would never be permitted in a standard subdivision, with its rigidly separated zoning categories.

Besides the feeling of community, retirees Luke and Marjorie Lamb like having less house and yard to maintain. Their airy 1,700-square foot home, designed by their architect son-in-law, is on a narrow, 50-by-120-foot lot—a nice compromise, they say, between a typical suburban house and a condo or apartment.

If the Lambs, both 67, get to the point where even a compact house is too much to take care of, a 55-unit condominium for senior citizens is under construction nearby. Townhouses and live/work units are also under way. Within 10 years, the subdivision is expected to have 400 single-family homes and another couple of hundred condo and apartment units and live/work spaces—the kind of mix that New Urbanists advocate. Open spaces, including 44 acres of trails and wetlands, all are within walking distance.

The community was planned by an internationally known husband-and-wife team of architects, Andres Duany and Elizabeth Plater-Zyberk. The houses, lots included, sell from $150,000 to $450,000. And, reflecting the late Marshall Erdman's association with Frank Lloyd Wright, all are built in the Prairie, Bungalow or Craftsman styles, with broad horizontal lines and low, overhanging roofs—a consistency that some critics find a bit monotonous but the Erdman folks defend as harmonious.

An hour-and-a-half away is another, more affordable New Urbanist development—Milwaukee's CityHomes—that planners say may be more typical of where the movement is headed: reclaiming abandoned or underutilized sites within the city, instead of plowing new ground in suburban areas. Bordered by W. Walnut, N. 23rd, Brown and N. 19th streets, the subdivision was begun by the city four years ago on cleared land.

CityHomes shares with Middleton Hills a pedestrian-friendly compactness. With its tidy alleys and attractive rows of simplified Queen Anne houses, all with porches, the streetscapes have an old-fashioned rhythm and comforting scale; its streets feature landscaped traffic islands that slow down cars and add green space.

As at Middleton Hills, CityHomes' residents sing the praises of neo-traditional planning. Listen to Renita Roberson, 30, a Milwaukee Public School teacher who recently moved into her spanking new home with her 34-year-old fiance, Marlon Teague, a contractor: "You're real close to your neighbors, and that's a blessing. They look out for you. If the people who live behind me see me coming home late at night, they watch and wave. There's a feel of family around here."

That habit of neighbors looking out for neighbors, combined with home security systems, has made residents feel unusually safe in an area that was once pretty rough.

CityHomes' middle-class residents could afford to live in the suburbs. But many have ties to this neighborhood; some have parents living nearby. Others, like Darius and Jennifer Wright—he's a civil engineer, she's a transportation engineer—like living close to their jobs. The Wrights also figure that they got more house for the money than they would have in the suburbs; even with extras, their handsome three-bedroom cost just $100,000.

Many homeowners here sense that they are on the cutting edge of an urban renaissance. "It's an up-and-coming area, and I wanted to be a part of it," says Charlotte Lawson, who lives in the development with her husband, Terence, and their two children.

With base models selling for $90,000 to $95,000, including the lot, the 43 homes were snapped up almost as soon as they became available; there's a 300-person waiting list for the next 25 houses on adjacent blocks. Assessed value in the surrounding area has gone up by 13%, and Wisconsin Housing and Economic Development Authority and Habitat for Humanity are building moderately priced homes on empty lots nearby. What's missing, except for a nearby Sentry supermarket and a McDonald's, is retail. But that's expected to grow along with home-ownership.

Meanwhile, a neighborhood tattered by years of disinvestment and neglect is getting a new lease on life—house by house, block by block. That, say its advocates, is what New Urbanism is all about.

Whitney Gould lives in Milwaukee and is the urban landscape writer for the *Milwaukee Journal Sentinel*.

new york city: port of my re-entry

ben logan

Editor's note: Most people know Ben Logan from his beautiful account of growing up on his family farm in Wisconsin's southwestern corner. However, Mr. Logan has also spent much of his life in our country's biggest city, New York. Although the following essay is about New York City, it explains why cities, no matter where they are, are such rich and important places—they provide us the opportunity to discover the powerful connections that occur with increased human contact.

When I look back at all the stories of my life, I am struck by the knowledge that places become living characters. I interact with and am shaped by places just as I am by human characters. Person and place become intertwined.

I was hill-born into the twisted, tumbling land of southwestern Wisconsin. The word "urban" was not in my vocabulary. Little towns with a few hundred persons were my cities, an easy transition from our hilltop farm.

During World War II, there was a parade of cities—Algiers, Tunis, Palermo, Salerno, Naples, Anzio—a series of dots on maps along the North African coast, across Sicily, then north on the Italian mainland. Those cities were not places at all, just symbols of death and destruction. War itself became the dominating place and character in my life.

Yet—and I had almost forgotten—there were smaller cities in Italy where fading light softened the harsh lines of wounded buildings. Bonfires flickered in the shattered streets. Italians—mostly children and older people—gathered around the fires and sometimes there were voices in song, a hint that even here in the ruins there was a fragile promise that humanity would survive.

New York City was my re-entry point after three years of war. It was a transition place. I was angry at first. The city was too untouched by death and the tragic comedies of war. Surely the city had its own hidden human wounds, but for a time it seemed to me that New York did not know there had been a war. The very normality of peacetime filled me with a sense of having lost a rare Camelot moment when self-interest had been put aside.

 There was a half-facetious bitterness in many who returned from overseas. On Eighth Avenue one morning I met a man I had known in Italy, an editor of the GI newspaper, *Stars And Stripes*. We shook hands rather awkwardly as though we had become strangers in this alien place called New York City. I told him I was still in the Navy and was trying to come all the way home. He told me he was editing a magazine for the Hearst Corporation. "I'm paid fifteen thousand a year," he said, "and all I have to do is sell my soul every day." We shook hands again and he went into the Hearst building.

As the months went by, New York began to be my city, revealing itself to me in stories and incidents that came from outside myself. My naval duties included helping hospitalized veterans who were interested in writing. Commuter trains and subways became part of my life. Broadway Theater and the museums filled a neglected niche in me that I had not known was there. I walked the city for hours and at all hours. New York was unbelievably safe then, and I again encountered the power of softening light and darkness. People acquainted with the night appeared, willing to be open and free as though nighttime pushes aside barriers that stand between us in the unforgiving light of day. I was told of a New York street photographer who said there are a million stories in the Naked City.

I found some of those stories.

Many nights I walked across the Brooklyn Bridge, finding an odd pleasure in standing at the middle of the bridge at midnight, noise of the city hushed, the vastness reduced to tiny vignettes. Several times I talked with a young woman who also walked the bridge at night. She was trying to find some feel or essence or even the ghost of Thomas Wolfe, a writer who had died in 1938. He, too, had had a special feel for the Bridge. She told me he had once written that only the dead know Brooklyn and that even they don't know it through and through. After several months she was gone from the bridge at night.

I became acquainted with the soapbox orators of Union Square and Columbus Circle. They came in early evening, lugging their boxes, and waited for a chance to speak. There were anarchists, socialists, communists, free thinkers, Bible thumpers, flag wavers, peace advocates, war advocates, labor union supporters, philosophers and others who spoke on subjects too obscure to be categorized.

A writer friend, Arnold Schulman, often went with me to hear the orators. He had an offbeat turn of mind him-self and kept saying he was going to speak some night. I found a wooden box for him and he invented "Balance-ism." Carrying his box, he went to Columbus Circle and delivered his new philosophy with great authority. All I remember now is his claim that every happening causes a counter-balancing happening, which reduces every-thing again and again to the starting point. He received enthusiastic applause.

The same night Arnold spoke, the Columbus Circle shoeshine man, who was mute, borrowed a box, climbed onto it and gave a speech in pantomime with many gestures. The boisterous crowd quieted. When the man made a final eloquent gesture, there was prolonged applause. He bowed very gracefully, stepped down from the box, picked up his shoeshine equipment and returned to his usual place on the sidewalk.

The glimpses and stories of New York City continued to blow around me. On Third Avenue one night I was stopped by a small, thin, pixie-faced man who very politely suggested I might be interested in loaning him two dollars which he promised never to return. He also volunteered that he has just been released from prison on Riker's Island.

"In prison for what?" I asked.

He laughed. "I drink. Sometimes when I drink, I behave inappropriately. That's what the judge keeps telling me. You going to let me have two dollars?"

I shook my head.

"Well," he said, "I hate to do this but I want to tell you I'm a terrible singer and I'm going to follow you down the street, singing to you 'til you come up with two bucks."

I handed him two one-dollar bills. "I see you're new at this," he said. With an elegant flourish, he handed me back one of the bills.

One morning on Madison Avenue a young woman was walking ahead of me. She was wearing a severely plain suit and carrying a briefcase. As we detoured away from a construction project, one of her high heels went into a crack on the boardwalk and broke off. She hobbled on a few steps, then stopped and took off the other shoe.

She looked at it a moment, then went back, stuck the heel of the good shoe into the crack and snapped it off to match the broken one. The men at the construction site had stopped working to watch her. They yelled their approval. She waved to them, picked up her briefcase and walked on as though nothing had happened.

Years later I remembered those illustrations of the irrepressible spirit of New Yorkers when Mayor John Lindsay was a guest on a radio program I was producing. "Nobody runs New York City," he said. "Yesterday I was walking across 42nd Street and a fire truck came by, horn blowing. I called to the fireman hanging on at the back and asked where the fire was. He waved and yelled, 'No fire, your honor. Just going out for coffee and bagels.' "

The day I left New York, I knew what was going to happen. As I walked to my car, I would go past Harry, the old man who sold newspapers at the corner of 57th Street and Eighth Avenue, and he would say, "Where you going this time, Boy?" He did that and I said, "I'm going to Wisconsin, Harry." He nodded, as he always did, and said, as he always did, "You do that, Boy. You go there. That's a good place."

But the City would not release me that easily.

In North Africa, during the war, a French woman had told me there are places one can never truly leave. For me, New York City became such a place. It has many times called me back from far wanderings and country life. Each time, the City reclaims me. Each time, I feel instantly at home.

Ben Logan is well-known Wisconsin author of *The Land Remembers, The Empty Meadow, A Christmas Remembered* and many other books. His books not only transport us, they impress upon us the importance of people and place to one's identity.

olbrich botanical gardens

jerry minnich

In the history and scope of public gardens, the Olbrich Botanical Gardens, in Madison, do not loom large. Pennsylvania's Longwood Gardens, Cranbrook in Michigan, even the Boerner Gardens in Milwaukee are much grander and better known.

But largeness is not the point of a public garden.

The point, I think—at least on the most personal level—is to establish a moment in time shared between observer and observed, a moment—or a series of moments—that serve to clear the mind and refresh the spirit, to bring everyday events into perspective, or even to wash them away for a brief time. After a day spent dealing with demanding clients, or riveting steel plates onto whatsit gizmos, or injecting the values of civilization into groups of reluctant children, a garden can provide a connection of a different kind.

To sit on a bench and contemplate a Monarch butterfly perched atop a Queen Anne's Lace flower cluster is to reduce life to manageable size, if only for a minute. And how easy is it to become lost in the babbling of a small stream over a single black rock?

On a larger scale, a public garden is certainly one of the noblest expressions of community in a democracy. It is a place of serenity and beauty accessible to prince and pauper alike, the blazing April daffodils giving no less golden a show for one than for the other. In this garden, for this moment, we are all equal.

I grew to love the Olbrich Botanical Gardens as soon as I moved to Madison some 35 years ago, and I have since had a chance to see them grow and prosper. I was surprised, in researching the history of the gardens the other day, to realize that I have been witness to more than half their life. Even though the genesis of the gardens goes back as far as 1916, when Michael Olbrich first dreamed the dream, it was not until 1952 that the first structures were built. The Olbrich Botanical Society was not incorporated until 1979, and the gardens really have not come into appreciable flowering until the past decade. We won't talk about full flowering. That will take another 100 years.

Everyone who visits these gardens is the inheritor of a grand legacy, one begun by Michael Olbrich and, even earlier, by John Olin, who was the father of the Madison parks system. The legacy continues to the present day, with contributions of both time and money from literally thousands of people, from volunteers who weed the perennial beds, pot up chrysanthemums, and sell raffle tickets, to those who contribute funds through memberships and donations, to the major financial contributors—individuals, families, and corporations—that make possible quantum leaps in construction.

A garden is a common meeting ground between humankind and the natural world. It has also been described as *nature tamed*. Less recognized, perhaps, is that a garden is capable of taming us, as well. When I spend a lunch hour sitting by the Olbrich rock garden, or strolling among the perennials or herb gardens, my world is instantly tamed, not only for the time I am there but for the rest of the day. And on a frozen January day, when the snow is swirling outside and the wind sweeps down across Lake Mendota and through the Madison isthmus, I take brief refuge in the Bolz Conservatory, there to be surrounded instantly by tropical plants and birds, and the smell of fresh, moist earth. It doesn't get much more magical than that.

Public gardens are one of the rewards of city living. They have been, since classical times. Here in Madison, we are fortunate to have a young and growing public garden, perfectly in keeping with this young and growing city.

Five acres of adjoining land were recently added to the gardens, and plans are now under way for expansion into the additional space.

The legacy continues.

Jerry Minnich, who runs Prairie Oak Press, in Madison, is also the author of eight books, including the *Wisconsin Garden Guide,* **the** *Ohio Gardening Guide,* **and the** *Michigan Gardening Guide.* **Formerly an editor of** *Organic Gardening* **magazine, he has lived and worked in Madison since 1965.**

brent nicastro capitol groundskeeper hands a tulip to a passerby

the city at play

henry h. smith international snow sculpting competition, milwaukee

titletown and its packers

thomas m. olejniczak

Monday morning. The Packers lost a heartbreaking game to the Panthers yesterday. Fog permeates the area. School delays are broadcast over local radio stations. Shower with the radio announcer analyzing the game. Have breakfast and discuss lousy game with spouse. Stop at convenience store to grab a coffee for the ride in. Pat, Glen, Rod, Jim, all have an idea of what's wrong. Everyone is cranky. Get to the office. Nobody smiles. By noon the mood is more critical. "Why did the players play like that? Why didn't they try this? What about the time out?" Stop on the way home. "What ya gonna do about those Packers?" Get home. Dog quietly greets you. Spend quiet evening watching Monday Night Football with dog. It's this way all over the City. We live and die with, but love, our Pack.

The most unique franchise in the history of professional sports evolved from a marriage of interests between a group of football loving and playing individuals and the citizens of the city of Green Bay. When E.L. "Curly" Lambeau and George Calhoun took a fledgling group of enthusiastic young lads and created the "Packers" with the sponsorship of the Indian Packing Company in 1919, the citizens of Green Bay embraced the venture with an unparalleled commitment to its ongoing success. The Packers joined the NFL in 1921. In 1923, the first public stock offering was made, which tied the community to the Packers forever.

The game of American football, having evolved from its beginnings in the late 19th century, was part and parcel of the small American city atmosphere. It was during this period that interest in American football increased dramatically because of the number of participants at the high school and college level, and the success that college football enjoyed. With the graduation of many fine players who enjoyed the unique sport because of its team concept, teams such as the Packers became popular outlets for the talents of gridiron heros. Cities like Canton, Decatur, Duluth, Green Bay and Dayton thoroughly embraced their Bulldogs, Staleys, Eskimos, Packers and Triangles. These towns, and others like them, put together a loose-knit network of exhibitions which caught the interest of the American heartland.

Perhaps it was befitting because of the involvement of Calhoun and Andrew Turnbull, who were the sports editor and business manager of the *Green Bay Press Gazette*, that the Packers received a greater share of publicity than other local sports ventures. Clearly, from the large crowds that ringed Hagemeister Park, the adventure created a stir within the city of Green Bay. City Stadium opened in 1925 next to East High School, the result of a partnership among the Packers, the city and the school board. In 1957, Lambeau Field was opened, the result of a partnership between the city and the Packers.

While the early days pale in comparison to the money involved today, the passion and enthusiasm of fans and players remained a benchmark for which other teams strived. Passing the hat was the common way for the fans to show their appreciation for the players, and the players' salaries in large measure came from this type of unstructured admission policy. Green Bay's reputation was as a hardworking, manufacturing community. People worked hard in their endeavors and greatly enjoyed the community feeling that came from cheering on their own

Packers. The Packers didn't disappoint, winning three League Championships for their fans.

When an unfortunate accident in which a fan fell from the stands occurred in 1931, putting the team on the brink of insolvency, it was the citizens of Green Bay who stepped forward to raise enough money to keep the franchise afloat. A second stock offering was made in 1935, when the original corporation went into receivership during the Depression.

Subsequently, the team enjoyed success in the late '30s and early '40s when the "Herber-to-Hudson" combination elevated the forward pass to the forefront and laid the foundation for the modern game we know today. Three more championships were added by the Packers during this era.

The late '40s saw a financial and playing downturn for the Packers. A Thanksgiving Day Intra-squad Game was needed to raise money. The community responded by raising nearly $50,000 to keep the team afloat. Subsequently, another stock offering in 1950 further cemented the town-team relationship. Until 1997, the shareholders of the 1950 offering elected the board of directors which oversaw the winning of five World Championships during the Packers' "Glory Years." It was during this era that Green Bay became known as "Titletown, U.S.A.." The organization had always been managed by a community-involved board, and to this day requires that a majority of the board members live in Brown County.

The commercial impact of the relationship has also grown immensely over time. There are over 57 businesses which capitalize on the "Packer" or "Titletown" themes in the area. The economic impact of the Packers on the city is estimated at over $145 million per year. The sheer volume of fans which descend upon the stadium area on Packer Sunday creates a surreal atmosphere which is unparalleled in the National Football League.

Most importantly, however, is the emotional tie that binds the citizenry and the Packer team. Win on Sunday, and Monday is as rosy as a beautiful summer day. Lose, however, and Monday is as gloomy and dreary as the middle of January. We may criticize our Packers, but beware if any outsider does! We embrace the players, coaches and staff as if they had lived here all their lives. For when they arrive, they forever become a fabric of life in this city.

Thomas M. Olejniczak is a lifelong resident of Green Bay. He has served on the Packers' Board of Directors since 1986, is a partner in the law firm of Liebmann, Conway, Olejniciak & Jerry, SC and is the Chairman of the Board at St. Norbert College. He and his lovely wife of 28 years have two children—one attending law school at the University of Wisconsin-Madison and one a senior at St. Thomas University in St. Paul, Minnesota.

the people's park
Reprinted from Milwaukee Magazine, June 1998

bruce murphy

America's sportswriters had never seen anything like it. One of them dubbed Milwaukee County Stadium "an insane asylum with bases." Another suggested the fans behaved like "children attending their first circus."

Major-league baseball had arrived here with the opening of County Stadium, whose construction convinced the Boston Braves to move to Milwaukee in 1953, and the citizenry went bonkers. There were 12,000 screaming fans waiting at the train station when the Braves arrived here and 60,000 more lining the streets for a parade Downtown. The team's new fans showered the players with gifts—$100,000 in free cars, televisions, clothing and cheese.

At the stadium, long pop flies, even a vicious swing for a strike had the fans screaming with excitement. All that unsophisticated joy soon earned Milwaukee the title of "Bushville" from New York's hardened sportswriters.

Everyone in Milwaukee seemed united behind the Braves. The first season here set a league record in attendance, with 1.8 million fans. New records were set, culminating with 2.2 million fans in 1957. A *Sports Illustrated* cover story called it the "Milwaukee Miracle."

It was all made possible by the building of County Stadium. The idea went back to 1909, when parks activist Charles Whitnall suggested that the Menomonee Valley would be a suitable location. Actual planning began in the early 1940s.

The bickering over the proper site was reminiscent of the modern effort to replace County Stadium. Ten different locations were considered. There was even a "Downtown" site: the old Haymarket Square at Fourth and McKinley. In the end, the Menomonee Valley was chosen because it was centrally located, had lots of room for parking, and was served by the old rapid transit line. Alas, the service was disbanded by the time the ballpark opened.

The $5 million stadium was built by Osborn Engineering Co., the firm that had designed many ballparks, including Yankee Stadium and Fenway and Comiskey parks. Completed late in 1952, it was the first stadium built in America since 1934, and though less distinctive than some, it had the post-war feel of utter modernity that wowed its first viewers. Braves owner Lou Perini joined many in calling it "the newest and most modern in the country."

County Stadium was operated much like a public park, where for many years, fans were allowed to bring in their own six-packs. After one midnight doubleheader, stadium attendants were left with 60,000 empty beer cans to clean up.

The fans lived and died for their Braves, who would win the 1957 World Series, as Bushville beat New York. They suffered through the team's decline in the early 1960s and the heartbreaking loss of the Braves to Atlanta in 1965. They thrilled to Packers games during the Lombardi years and came back for baseball when the old Seattle Pilots became the Milwaukee Brewers in 1970. They cheered the pennant-winning Brewers who lost the World Series of 1982. And they celebrated the team's switch to the National League.

Soon, County Stadium will be replaced by a far fancier facility, Miller Park. But its creation, as in every other contemporary stadium, will also destroy a democratic ideal. The old ballparks were populist palaces where people from all walks of life rooted together for their team. The new stadiums' luxury boxes and club seats will ensure the wealthy never come near the rabble in the cheap seats or the throng waiting in line for their beers.

Miller Park could one day become the insane asylum that was County Stadium in 1953, but the inmates will never be as equal, or as blissfully united as those in that now quaint time when everyone was a proud citizen of Bushville.

Bruce Murphy is a Milwaukee writer and consultant. He is the former editor of the weekly newspaper, *Metro*, and former senior editor of *Milwaukee Magazine*.

red hot red, the wizard of waukesha

will kort

On August 11, 1998, a seven-mile stretch of state highway near the city of Waukesha was officially designated the Les Paul Parkway to honor its namesake—guitarist, inventor and Rock and Roll Hall of Fame inductee. Other sites considered for the tribute due to their historical significance were W. St. Paul Avenue – the location of Les Paul's boyhood home, and Williams St.—the location of Club 400, a tavern originally owned by his father, George Polfuss, where Les Paul did some of his earlier playing.

Waukesha has such a fondness for this man that a decade before the highway donned his name, Waukesha renamed the bandshell where he used to entertain as a teen-ager the Les Paul Performance Center. Part of the festivities included declaring the day of the dedication, March 30, "Les Paul Day" in Wisconsin. Representatives from the Wisconsin Area Music Industry presented Paul with the WAMI "Hall of Fame" award that he had won the previous November.

The roots of Les Paul's innovations can be traced to audio experiments he began conducting as a teen, when he was known by Waukesha locals as Red Hot Red—the redhead who would turn up around town with his two-sided harmonica and Sears, Roebuck Troubador guitar. Demonstrating his deftness as a self-taught electronics expert, the debut of his first amplified guitar took place at a drive-in barbecue stand at Goerkes Corners. Realizing that people in their cars were not able to hear his music, he took a radio and a transducer from a telephone mouthpiece and played the guitar through the radio. Attracting listeners from businesses across the road, Paul's audio experiment tripled his tips.

Although credited with countless achievements as both a performer and innovator, it is his fame as the pioneer of the solid body electric guitar and multitrack recording that place him in a category of his own. Although Les Paul is renowned as the pioneer of the solid body electric guitar, the historical record does not allow us to identify a single inventor of that instrument. Its evolution was the product of many minds working concurrently along similar paths. Electric guitars, including a solid body model, had been in existence since the 1920s. But most people in the guitar business, and most musicians, considered the solid body instruments a curiosity. Les Paul, already a well-known musician in Chicago's jazz clubs, tried to address the problem of feedback in the electric instruments of the period by having some solid body guitars produced to his specifications in the 1930s.

Like most visionaries, Paul was ahead of his time, and the guitar makers he enlisted didn't think much of the instrument's possibilities. Paul kept experimenting, and by 1941 had designed and built the Log, a prototypical solid body electric guitar that was fashioned from a simple board attached to a guitar neck. In 1949, he showed it to the conservative Gibson Guitar Company, then dominant in the nation's electric guitar business, but they turned him down. It wasn't until 1952 that Gibson signed him up and produced the first Les Paul model, at last giving respectability to the new instrument. The rest is history, as Les Paul models are consistently sought out by players and collectors as some of the most coveted electric guitars ever produced. The combination of Paul's prominence as a musician, his persistent belief in the solid body electric guitar, and his relationship with Gibson had finally ushered in a new era for popular music.

Les Paul's genius lay in the recognition that the solid body electric guitar was not simply a louder guitar, but an entirely new instrument with profound expressive capabilities. Even though Les Paul also pioneered the use of guitar "effects," he could not have imagined all of the devices that would eventually be introduced to modify the sound of the electric guitar, ranging from wah-wah pedals and distortion boxes to guitar synthesizers, and including techniques like feedback and stereo splitting. The unique sounds of the electric solid body guitar and bass were integral to the evolution of rock and roll, jazz and blues from the '50s on, and it's hard to imagine newer forms like ska and reggae without the distinctive clipped chords of the solid body electric rhythm guitars.

If Bo Diddley gave rock music its rhythm, Les Paul gave it its voice. Of course, rock and roll is as much about style and attitude as music, and here the solid bodies had a distinct advantage. Style and substance came together in the big semi-hollow body electrics favored by rockabilly guitarists, prized as much for their looks as for their sound, which was midway between acoustic and solid body electric.

As influential as Les Paul was in the development and eventual popularity of the solid body electric guitar and its effects, he pioneered several recording techniques that arguably had an even more profound effect on the way music is created and experienced.

Along with the techniques of reverb and overdubbing, multitrack recording was a musical revolution that in many ways mirrored that of the solid body electric guitar.

Multitracking is the technique of using multiple microphones, one (or more) for each musician, or a direct feed in the case of electric instruments, to capture the sounds. Then these separate "tracks" are combined, or mixed, allowing much greater creative control of the finished recording. Certain tracks of a recording may be punched up in volume, compressed, limited and altered in countless other ways to achieve a particular sound far removed from the original. A single musician can now play and record every instrument on a recording, and different parts of a song can be recorded at different times, in different cities, by people who have never met. Things that are impossible in the acoustical real world can be conceived and created with the mixing board.

Today, virtually all music recordings, movie soundtracks and most live concerts are produced using the methods pioneered by Les Paul. Some genres, such as hip-hop and techno, are completely dependent on these techniques, and the continuing evolution of surround sound is based on them. His influence will continue well into the next century and beyond.

Les Paul's contributions to the current pop sound will continue to be commemorated not only by his hometown, but by the world at large. In November 1996, the Smithsonian completed the exhibit, "From Frying Pan to Flying V: The Rise of the Electric Guitar." New York City, where Les Paul at 85 still performs, has been considered as a possible site at which to establish a Les Paul museum. One cannot tune in to the airwaves, listen to a CD or attend a concert today without experiencing firsthand the innovations of Waukesha's best-known son.

Will Kort is a Milwaukee-based writer and audiophile.

junior optimist club red hot rag time band—mid 1920s (les paul is standing second from the right)

untitled

susan firer

A night game in Menomonie Park
where the ladies hit the large white balls
like stars through the night they roll
like angelfood cake batter folded through devilsfood.
Again, I want to hear the fans' empty beer cans
being crushed—new ones hissing open.
"You're a gun, Anna."
"She can't hit."
"Lay it on."
Oh run swift softball women
under the lights the Kiwanis put in.
Be the wonderful sliding night
animals I remember. Remind me constantly
of human error and redemption.
Hit
ball after ball to the lip of the field
while the lake flies fall like confetti
under the park's night lights.
Sunlight Dairy team, remember me
as you lift your bats,
pump energy into
them bats whirling circular as helicopter
blades above your heads.
Was it the ball Julie on the "Honey B" Tavern team
hit toward my head that made me so softball crazy that right in the middle of a tune
by Gentleman Jim's Orchestra, here in Bingo/Polka
Heaven at Saint Mary of Czestochowa's annual Kielbasa
Festival, I go homesick for Oshkosh women's softball?
I order another kielbasa and wonder
if Donna will stay on third next game or

again run head-down wild into Menomonie homeplate?
Play louder, Gentleman Jim,
Saint Mary of Czestochowa throws a swell festival, but
Oshkosh women's softball—that's the whole other ballgame.

Susan Firer lives in Milwaukee. Her third book of poems, T*he Lives of Saints and Everything*, won the Cleveland State University Poetry Center Prize and the Posner Award. "Untitled" originally appeared in *The Underground Communion Rail* (1992).

henry h. smith **sonny rollins, miller stage—summerfest**

william hurrle

I'm on the porch on a midsummer Friday night. Our farm, on the outskirts of Green Bay, is the dream scene for many city dwellers, but it is constant labor. Property is the enemy of leisure. There's a leased field of crops and chemicals to the west and south, and a hay field to the east of our five-acre farmstead. To the immediate north, Highway 54 roars and whines. The lights of Green Bay light up the western night sky, and leapfrogging sprawl has spewed pockets of suburbs along county roads all around us. Even the chemical field is zoned "transitional agriculture"; we could wake up one morning looking at the dumpster-end of a strip mall.

The moon is waxing. If we still lived in the city I'd be on my bicycle, easing through cool air, through neighborhood streets with moms calling in even the big kids, slipping off to cold beer and hot music in a joint such as Heroes in Green Bay, the old Humping Hannah's on the East Side of Milwaukee, Clark Kent's Super Joint with Dale Kuipers' art or C.J. Mack's, both on Main St. in Green Bay, or the Crystal Corner in Madison. There are others such as Bill Nolte's The Joint on Water Street in Eau Claire, UWGB's old Blue Whale Coffeehouse, UW-Madison's Memorial Union Rathskeller, Emmitt's in Appleton, the Silver Moon in Darien, Mr. G's in Door County, the Up & Under and Mamie's in Milwaukee now, and venues too many and ephemeral to mention that host the music.

Country distances are too large, destinations too few, to use a bike. My little pick-up would get me the 24 miles to Heroes in 15 minutes for about $10, including the price of gas, depreciation, insurance, etc. The cost would be at least double that counting pollution, defense of Arabian reserves, depletion allowance, tax breaks for oil corporations, public health declines, etc. But the Toyota isn't silent, isn't sensual, and the law lurks at the end of the night. Cops don't give bicycles a second look at bar time. They are busy with fights, wrecks and disturbing the peace calls. A bicycle slips through the dark streets, a wee packet of awareness, with no more impact than a falling leaf. Cars pinch the senses and lessen the human measure.

At the joint, a smooth dismount and parking near the door. A quick lock up and into the scene as the band warms up with the first set. My idea of good music is the place where blues, jazz and folk meet. Wisconsin is just a step away from Chicago, between Minneapolis and Detroit. Touring bands are happy to get off the bus, play music and make some fans and friends. They like the Wisconsin ambience. It is different, more laid back, more tolerant. In lots of places a night out is honky tonkin'—whisky drinking, fights and cheating sex—SIN! In Wisconsin it is a few beers, talking and dancing with friends, socializing. A night out in a Wisconsin blues joint is not about machismo and sex. It is about music and community.

Dancing to the blues is ecstasy, rapture, transport beyond the bounds of self. At its best this mix of energy builds to an intensity that overcomes individual existence. The dancing bodies move so fast and take up so much space there is no longer room for individual expression. Psychologically, there is so much unity within the music the dancers become one in it. I remember nights in Oshkosh's old Wage Peace where dancers would throw their arms around each other to form lines, high-kicking in spontaneous unison to Blue Tail Fly's music. Usually the women start it.

Wisconsin blues joints are different in another way, too. There is gender equality and openness. The first dancers on the floor are often a couple of women, friends out for a night. Nobody thinks anything of it. Some people get up and dance alone. But really they're not. They are dancing with the band, with the music, with the ghosts of ancestors. When there is lots of eye contact between dancers, and dancers and musicians, it is going to be a good night. Dancing and bicycling go together. They both want leg and lung strength. Fuel, too. Beers keep dehydration at bay and lift the mood, but don't damage coordination needed to dance and to balance on the bike ride home.

Not everyone gets into blues and dancing. It is a cultural subset, a small civil religion that empowers people. Dancing to the blues has little to do with the market and control centers our cities have become. Music is dematerialism refined, and the blues is a dialogue, a call and response between musicians and audience, especially dancers. Dialogue is what cities are really about. Sharing in the music is a reprise of sanity, a reaffirmation of the celebratory impulses that first brought people together in cities millennia ago.

The bike ride home through the city streets is especially delicious: the soft rush of cool air, the steady pedaling rhythm, the intimacy of the road surface, of leaning through corners, pumping up and down hills, past windows and doorways that beckon with tales of other lives. And because they're Wisconsin city streets, there are natural delights—the cathedral of street trees, the smell of lakes and rivers, the moon and stars and the sweet wine of night air. After the amped-up communal celebration, riding through the dark silence centers me in a private, peaceful place. I miss both city joys.

Bill Hurrle is a contractor specializing in conservation and renewable energy. He has written for years as a small press activist. He loves bicycles, Wisconsin and the blues.

civil disobedience by dawn's early light

Reprinted from Milwaukee Journal Sentinel, December 18, 1994

vince vukelich

I want to confess. I violated Milwaukee Code of Ordinances Section 105-21 today. I wasn't planning on committing this act, so at least nobody can accuse me of doing it with malice aforethought.

I was walking to work, as I usually do, somewhat dumbly watching the world come into focus around me. When I leave my house at about 6 a.m., it is fairly dark, but as I make my way through the streets of my Riverwest neighborhood, the sky starts to lighten. The streetlights pulse for a brief second and then go off for the day. The sunrise is now after 7 a.m. By then the eastern sky turns a wonderful orange just before the sun breaks through. And I let my mind wander through aimless thoughts, stray poems and abandoned lyrics. I allow my eyes to randomly dart in and out of the darkened alleys, detecting danger and adventure, both real and imagined, lurking in every shadow.

On clear mornings, or at least semi-cloudless ones, I will try to make my way to Reservoir Park, which provides a wonderful view of the eastern horizon and the silhouettes of the buildings downtown.

Today, as I veered to the left from the sidewalk on North Avenue, onto the sidewalk that leads through the park, I looked up at the sign at the park's entrance:

> **ALL RECREATIONAL ACTIVITIES ARE**
> **PROHIBITED IN THIS PUBLIC AREA**
> **BETWEEN 10:00 P.M. AND 8:00 A.M.**
> **IN ACCORDANCE WITH MILWAUKEE CODE OF**
> **ORDINANCES SECTION 105-21**

I walked on, focusing on my goal, concentrating on reaching my work destination, attempting to keep any thoughts of random recreating out of my mind. ("Book him, Danno—premeditated recreation one.") I walked by the soccer field, past the small shelter with the gang graffiti on the outer walls, up the small hill to the area where several large oaks and birch trees are gathered. The trees, ever patient, would not let me pass. They forced me to turn around, and I did. I saw the dark black clouds sitting heavily on the horizon, back-lit by a spectacular orange light bursting forth and spilling golden residue on the sleeping city around me. I lost my focus. I no longer cared about my destination, and I'm not sure, for those brief moments, if I even had one.

Out there in the open, on the top of a hill across the Milwaukee River from the abandoned A.F. Gallun Tannery, exposed to the biting wind on a 30-degree late autumn morning, with only a vague awareness of the world beyond my immediate senses, more in tune with a universal serenity that any human-made comfort, without any remote-control, gas-powered, artificially sweetened, new and improved, titanium-shafted, mechanized cordless contrivance, apparatus or gizmo, I was recreating. Shamelessly. Brazenly. Defiantly.

And although I had no intention of committing such a disgraceful act when I walked into the park at 6:36 this Thursday morning on the first day of December, I want to state categorically and unequivocally right here and now … as long as there is one patch of concrete-free ground, as long as there is one tree to shield my body from wind and rain, as long as there is one drop of water in the river below to reflect the full moon, as long as there is a sun to bathe my soul in reflective light…I will recreate in that park again. Even between the hours of 10 p.m. and 8 a.m.

Vince Vukelich lives in Milwaukee. He is an attorney with the U.S. Department of Agriculture working on natural resource issues with the Eastern Region of the Forest Service. He also serves on the board of the Urban Ecology Center, which provides environmental education and stewardship opportunities based in Riverside Park in Milwaukee.

thairath khanthavong curious joe

city excursions

mary jo walicki crosscountry skiers at minooka park in waukesha

urban cool and the city wild: three vignettes

judith strasser

My first Christmas in Madison, Lake Mendota clicked shut during a hard, cold, snowless spell. My new husband, Steve, was thrilled. "This doesn't happen very often," he told me, "but when it does, there's nothing like it. Can you skate?" I could, though not very well. But Steve infected me with his enthusiasm for a skating expedition. We rooted around in his mother's attic and found Steve's old hockey skates and a pair of his dad's black figure skates that more or less fit me. We made a Thermos full of cocoa, and drove along the lakeshore near the University.

We parked near the student union, carried the skates down to the lake, and sat on rocks to put them on. My ankles wobbled terribly as I stepped over the chunky mix of ice and pebbles at the water's edge. I clung to Steve. But in only a few feet, we were launched onto the glistening lake. The surface was extraordinary: smooth as glass. In some places, the ice was so clear you could see straight through it, four or five inches, to the watery world beneath. Feathery lake weeds floated under our feet. I imagined I saw a fish. Other places, thousands of tiny frozen bubbles turned the ice opaque. I got my "ice legs," stroked and glided, headed away from land. The university buildings shrank; the afternoon sun melted an invisible, slippery layer between our skate blades and the ice.

Suddenly, we came to a barrier: a place where the ice had buckled and broken. Uplifted sheets, big shards and blocks, piled like rubble, blocked our way. "An expansion crack," Steve explained. "Listen. You can hear it boom." The crack extended, parallel to the shore, as far as I could see. Several feet high, several feet wide, lapped in places by open water, it looked perilous. I followed Steve as he skated along it, looking for a way across. He found a place where it narrowed and helped me over, holding my arm to steady me. Beyond the crack, smooth ice stretched forever. I felt lucky. More than lucky: exalted. It seemed entirely possible to glide the whole ten miles to the opposite shore.

* * * * *

On a late-winter walk through Hoyt Park, I came across three little boys, eight or nine years old, marching single-file through the woods. The leader sang, "The bear went over the mountain ... Sound off!" His troops called out: "One." "Two." "The bear went over the mountain ..." "One." "Two." They stopped when they saw me, ducked behind the crest of the hill. I continued up the road and arrived at the overlook about the same time they emerged from the woods. The leader opened his khaki knapsack and handed out Fig Newtons. I tried not to scare them off; looked straight out over the city, pretended they weren't there. The boys hoisted themselves up to the stone wall and sat, dangling their legs, looking over the leafless trees at the sprawling expanse of Hilldale Mall; the houses set on tidy plots; the state office building where, in a few years, they would take their driving tests. The city sparkled in the sun. "This is so cool," one of them said, and it was.

* * * * *

A year or two ago, on Memorial Day, I tried to hike around Lake Wingra without walking on a road. I struck out into the woods behind the boathouse. Purple and white violets lined the path. I passed the duck pond, followed the trail through the oak savanna—and then it petered out. I found myself in a broad expanse of downed and matted reeds, walking on a mat of rushes laid over hillocks and stubble. In the distance, a young man trained binoculars on a hawk. He heard the crackling reeds, saw me coming, moved away.

I headed into a marshy wetland. Thickets of willows, a meadow blooming with pink shooting stars. I headed for traces that changed, as I approached, into small streams and rivulets. I jumped across, or walked the banks until I found a few stepping stones. I favored high ground, guessed at directions, circled back on myself. I knew I couldn't get lost: I could hear the traffic. But I felt like an explorer, making my way through a wilderness.

Soon the willow thickets grew too thick to breach. Mounds of moss and clumps of marsh marigolds formed islands on a sea of black muck. Mats of watercress clogged the flowing rivulets. I had to cross a swamp: neither water nor land. I balanced on brittle bridges of shrubs; searched for footing on rotting tree stumps, mounds of bog plants, abandoned beaver dams. When I misjudged the depth of vegetation, or could not stretch my stride far enough, the muck oozed over my boot tops, sucked me in.

Grabbing at branches for balance, I crossed another stream, pushed through some willows, and found a walk made of planks and two-by-fours. I had entered the Arboretum. A couple in tennis shoes eyed my boots, the mud-streaked cuffs of my jeans. "Taking the hard way?" they laughed.

I shook my head. "Circumnavigating Lake Wingra." Surrounded by city, deep in the wild, buoyed by the skin of the earth.

Judith Strasser is an interviewer for "To The Best Of Our Knowledge," a nationally syndicated program produced by Wisconsin Public Radio. Her poetry has appeared in many literary magazines. "Urban Cool and the City Wild: Three Vignettes" has been excerpted from her memoir, *Black Eye*.

paul hayes

Leaving our house through its front door on Cedarburg's Columbia Road, I have choices.

If I turn right and walk for five minutes, I reach the bank, which holds our mortgage, our checking account and some of our savings. On the way, I pass 46 of the 82 structures on Columbia Road, the oldest of which was built in 1855 and the newest of which is under construction 145 years later.

I pass the little cooperage, where the late Adam Gleitzmann, who lived in a stone house next door, made oak barrels in the mid-19th century for the Weber Brewery. The stone cooperage was remodeled 20 years ago into a residence that looks for all the world like a cottage in Cornwall.

I pass Tom and Patty's new house, which Tom and their son, Alex, are building in the vacant lot next to their present, old house. On either side of the stone lintel over the door are two dates, 1999 A. D. and 156 B. E., the latter date informing us that we are in the 156th year of the Bahai Era, revealing the beliefs therein.

At the bank, which stands on the site of the old Columbia Mill, I know many of the bank employees by their first names. One of them, Gerry, leads my wife Philia's early morning aerobics class at the old high school gym, a 10-minute walk from our house in the other direction.

If I leave our house through its back door, I walk through our back yard to the banks of Cedar Creek, then along the creek through three other back yards, Al and Linda's, Steve's and Dellie's. That takes me to Adlai Horn Park, which features the Little League baseball diamond.

This is the first summer that Al and Linda are not living in their house next door. That's a major change on Columbia Road. Linda died last year at the age of 92. Now she lies under a headstone engraved with both their names in Zur Ruhe cemetery, which is a three-minute walk from my front door up a little spur street and across the old interurban right of way.

At 95, Al kept the flower garden going without Linda as best he could, clearing the leaves from the daffodils, weeding the lupines, uncovering the roses. "You got to keep going," he philosophized a couple of years ago as he leaned a ladder against his house so he could clean maple seeds from his gutters.

Al was born in a house on this very street, the house that Tom and Patty now live in. As a boy, when he and his brothers used to swim in the creek, the water ran clear and you could see the sandy bottom until you swam up to a cattail marsh where the park is now. Also, every year, the locals would cut ice from the creek to preserve food during the summer. Both swimming and harvesting ice would be unthinkable today. The water is far too polluted. But neighbors still use it for canoeing, paddle boating and ice-skating.

Al and Linda built their house in 1931, and in it they reared two daughters and nurtured Linda's mother, who lived upstairs until her death in the 1960s. But with Linda gone, the loneliness got to Al, and he would forget to eat and grew thin. Now, he's in a nursing home. Steve, next door down, bought his old Oldsmobile.

Dellie's house also is empty. Dellie lived there with his mother, and he took early retirement from a local industry because he had developed a thriving, home-owned business reloading ammunition used in target practice by the area police departments.

An unforgettable street party began at 3 a.m. one hot summer morning when Dellie's gunpowder storage shed blew up. Neighbors in pajamas and nightgowns poured out of their houses to watch the conflagration. Our volunteer fire department, three blocks away, arrived 45 minutes later, far too late to save the shed, which caused the neighbors to speculate that our firemen knew full well what was in the shed and saw little harm in letting it burn down a bit.

Dellie, too, has entered a time of bad health, and his house has been empty for a year or more. Steve, who works at Hoffmann's Meat Market, one of the few original businesses left in downtown Cedarburg, and who rents a flat in a duplex between the two empty houses, hopes to buy it.

If the Little Leaguers are playing, I can watch awhile from the aluminum bleachers. If not, I can continue down the path and across the footbridge over the creek, which places me in Cedar Creek Park, with its bandshell, its towering white ash trees, its chattering flock of inbred mallards and the playground.

The park's path takes me to the five-story Hilgen-Schroeder grist mill, built in 1855, and now Cedarburg's most impressive landmark, and next door to it, the 1920s red-roofed pagoda, one of the last of 100 such Chinese temples that distinguished the Wadham Oil Company's chain of service stations. Now it houses an artsy jewelry studio.

Here I am half a block from downtown Cedarburg, which basically is contained on Washington Avenue between St. Francis Borgia Catholic Church, built in 1870, on the south end of the street, and the Wittenberg Woolen Mill, built in 1864, about seven blocks northwest.

If I cross Washington and walk between the Washington House Bed and Breakfast and the cleaners, I reach the post office and the library. I often take clothes to the cleaners, stop in the library to read a paper and drop off our bills and letters at the post office in the same walk.

If I turn southeast on Washington, I come to the Coffee Pot, the restaurant where many decisions about preserving Cedarburg were made informally by the aldermen and the late Stephan Fischer, the stubborn mayor who refused to allow our historic buildings to be torn down 30 years ago. They wouldn't get by with that kind of rump session in today's legal climate, but no one's complaining about their results.

True, the old enterprises—groceries, pharmacies, hardware, men's clothing, paint and wallpaper, bakeries and the like—have been replaced with antique, craft, jewelry and specialty shops. But that's the commerce that has vindicated the wisdom of Fischer: new uses for old buildings.

Old-time Cedarburg residents bristle at the suggestion that their town is a suburb of Milwaukee. Its history proves otherwise. From its beginning, Cedarburg was a self-contained settlement, a milling, industrial and retail center that predates Wisconsin statehood.

Like a glacier, sprawl, with its isolated houses in cornfields, has advanced to Cedarburg's southern border. Now the glacier is splitting and moving around us on both sides, swallowing dairy farms and surrounding us with formless development. But in its midst stands a tight little island of tradition whose inhabitants work hard at maintaining an illusion.

Entering the 21st century, Cedarburg citizens strive for the rhythm and appearance of American life about 1900, a place and time wherein neighbors know each other and where most chores can be accomplished in a morning's walk.

Paul G. Hayes retired as an award winning environmental reporter for the Milwaukee Journal Sentinel in 1995. He lives in Cedarburg with his wife, Philia.

la crosse at a runner's pace

chris hardie

Sometimes I run.

I run for the exercise, but I also run for more. I run because I sweat, I cleanse, I think, I wonder. Sometimes I run from work—both literally and figuratively—when I take a break during a hectic shift. Life in the newsroom can clutter your mind and I need to retreat, reflect, renew and refresh.

And wonder.

It's early evening as I begin. Jogging slowly, I warm up my muscles. The swinging sounds of jazz float from the South Side Oktoberfest grounds, where it's opening night for the annual Great River Jazz Fest. Temptation bids me to stop and listen for a while. But I am resolved to continue running.

I approach Riverside Park, where there is more music from a band on the outdoor stage. I like the park because it draws people of all sorts, young and old, rich and poor—folks from all walks. I pass an elderly couple strolling hand-in-hand, looking very much in love. I smile. They smile back. Farther south in the park in the shade of a tree a younger couple in deep conversation sprawls on the grass. I wonder if they too, are in love.

Front Street is busy. It's wrestling night at the La Crosse Center. Two satellite television trucks send signals to broadcast live to the rest of the country. I wonder how many of the 5,000 fans of pugilism will wake up Friday morning with hoarse voices.

Sometimes I run up and over the Cass Street Bridge, winding my way through Pettibone Park. Tonight, I cross under the bridge and continue south down Front Street. At Front and Market, the street sign is half-covered by cardboard from a 12-pack of a discount beer not made by the big plant two blocks away. I wonder if this is someone's idea of a cruel joke or bitter irony.

I draw closer to the brewery, expecting at any second a waft of the sour, mashie smell of beer in the making. But tonight there is no smell. Breweries being shut down have to stop making beer. Several brewery workers are gathered in back of the brewery, sitting and standing among battered lunch pails. I wonder if it is their last work break together.

I turn through Houska Park just as a tow pushes several barges upriver. My pace picks up as the clink of an aluminum bat making contact with a softball drifts from the ball park. A tiny tot dashes through the park in barefoot glee, his watchful father close behind.

Moments later I cross the bridge, where just hours before an elderly man ended his life by jumping in the water. A shiver runs down my spine despite the pool of sweat that has formed on the small of my back.

Soon I will be halfway through my run. My feet cover the pavement in a steady and soothing rhythm. My breathing is slightly labored but comfortable. Exertion equals relaxation.

Muddy Flats is quiet in the evening, the industrial businesses closed for the night. I pass an apartment complex parking lot where a girl no more than three, wearing a tattered summer dress, plays basketball on a crooked toy hoop. She shoots and scores, a big grin spreading across her face when the scuffed ball passes through the plastic rim. I wonder if she will someday be on the cover of a sports magazine.

I pass another softball game at Green Island, where a deep drive to right center results in a triple with two runs scored. I head north past Gundersen Lutheran Medical Center. I admire those who comfort and heal the sick. I wonder how many will be healed tonight.

I cross South Avenue down Seventh Street. I pass a neighborhood bar, where a Neil Diamond song drifts from the open front door. An older man sits alone on the corner stool and takes a sip from a tap beer. I drink from the cool water at a bubbler at Seventh and Farnam. I wonder if the man on the stool is also looking for healing.

Near Hamilton Elementary School, I pass a group of laughing, smiling kids wearing orange shirts that reveal their involvement with the La Crosse Boys and Girls Club. One girl asks me as I pass if running is hard. "Naw," I reply. I am not convinced she believes me.

Near Seventh and Jackson a group of young kids plays in the yard. An older man, perhaps a father, grandfather or another relative, watches from the front porch steps. Soon it will be twilight, but the kids will probably play until dark, drinking in the sweetness of a summer night that seems to last forever.

At Becker Plaza some residents gather on the benches. They sit in the soft evening light, perhaps reflecting on summers gone by or wondering about their children and their children's children. I wonder if their children are thinking about them as well.

As I return to the heart of downtown, I am near the end of my run. The evening casts shadows upon the brick. It is quiet. Downtown is making its daily evolution— businessman by day, entertainer by night.

Near the courthouse I slow down and stop. The stream of water at the Third and Vine bubbler calls. I splash the cool water on my face and savor the sensation.

Several more steps and I'm back at the office. My run is over. The circuit is complete. My body is tired, yet alive. My mind is clear, yet full. The city has helped to rejuvenate me once again.

Chris Hardie is the local news editor for the *La Crosse Tribune*. This story appeared in his weekly column in the paper that features slice of life stories about life in the Coulee Region.

madison, by peddle and paddle

mike ivey

The Dudgeon-Monroe neighborhood is the kind of place new urbanists refer to when they talk dreamily of recreating the "traditional neighborhood." It's that classic mix of single-family homes and apartments, stores and shops, parks and walking paths—good living from America's best days.

My choice for getting around my neighborhood is by bike. It's under three miles from home to work, much of the way on a new city-funded asphalt path that follows the banks of Wingra Creek, a sluggish but healthy urban stream that connects Lake Wingra with Lake Monona. When newspapering takes me downtown to city hall and the Capitol, I can cover the three miles with a choice of paths. One gives a nice workout up the hill that is West Washington Avenue. (Remember, the Capitol is where it is because of that hill). The other passes through two parks and the two Mononas (Bay and Lake). A third still more special route allows me to ride home through the University of Wisconsin's Arboretum, a 1,280-acre research and restoration area established in 1934 with inspiration from planner John Nolen, funding through businessman Col. Joseph Jackson, and guidance from conservationist Aldo Leopold. While this route adds two miles to the trip, it's an easy trade-off, especially on summer days when the cooling shade from the hardwoods in the Arboretum's Galistel Woods offers a brief respite from Wisconsin's dress-shirt-soaking humidity.

Bike access isn't the only perk for an active lifestyle in the Dudgeon-Monroe neighborhood. Almost out my backdoor is Lake Wingra, where a ban on speedboats and an undeveloped shoreline make for some of the most pleasant paddling anywhere in the city. The marshy, southwest end of the lake is home to sandhill cranes, who have become so accustomed to curious canoeists they scarcely notice when paddlers approach. An assortment of other bird species also inhabit the lake, including the great blue and green herons. Migrating season brings through the occasional loon, egret and more varieties of colorful warblers than I can possibly identify.

Paddling to the other end of Lake Wingra brings you back to civilization; Edgewood College and Vilas Park with its beach and zoo. Farther east, anglers are usually casting from the shoreline, hoping to hook into one of the muskies that have taken off in Lake Wingra, thanks to help from the Department of Natural Resources. If you're intent on getting in a long paddle, portage around the spillway at the east end of Lake Wingra and continue down Wingra Creek. Local old-timers still refer to it as "Murphy's Crick," although nobody knows who Murphy was or why this is his crick.

When the water is high, like after a good rainstorm, you can actually paddle a canoe or small kayak all the way through to Olin Park, where the creek empties into Lake Monona. Continue south through the Yahara Chain of Lakes, you could theoretically paddle into the Rock River—which flows into the Mississippi River near Abilene. From Madison to New Orleans—my back yard to the French Quarter by canoe. Imagine that.

The bicyclists and paddlers have to share the neighborhood resources, of course. Runners get a gorgeous and varied 10-kilometer route around Lake Wingra through the Arboretum. And when winter arrives, the Arboretum offers some of the best cross-country skiing trails anywhere—let alone within a city with 200,000 residents. Madison's frozen lakes coax skaters to both Lake Wingra and the Vilas Park lagoon, where the city of Madison Parks Department tends the ice with tender loving care.

Of course, all that biking, running, paddling, hiking, skating and skiing is enough to work up a powerful thirst and a hearty appetite. That's OK. I've got a neighborhood tavern, three restaurants and a frozen custard stand within a block of home.

Mike Ivey is a columnist and reporter at *The Capital Times* in Madison. His work has appeared in a variety of regional publications from *Wisconsin Silent Sports* to the *Milwaukee Business Journal.*

brent nicastro madison seen through bike spokes

john fennell

It's a city of 628,000, but sometimes I am the only person here.

It is the noon hour in the middle of a busy week, and I have walked down Erie Street, past mammoth warehouses, past loading docks where paper rolls as big as compact cars are loaded onto flat-bed trucks.

As the street comes to an end, the sky, no longer blocked by brick, opens up into a panorama where a sea of gray asphalt meets the glistening river and ragged urban skyline.

To the east, the Hoan Bridge rises overhead, glowing like a fanciful sculpture with graceful arches and sinuous curves. Across the river, the sewage district's giant smokestack silently pumps endless pillows of white into the air. Across the watery expanse to the southwest, ladder-like arms of gravel-harvesting machinery stretch to meet the copper dome of St. Josephat in the distance. Looming above all is the western sky, the Allen-Bradley clock tower stands erect as a sentry on its watch.

Down the river, perched before the rising buildings of Downtown, an ancient railroad trestle carves black lines into an atmospheric tapestry of reds and grays, mauves and greens.

In spring, the fishermen join me. They sit in fold-up lawn chairs or stand next to their poles like figures in a Chinese watercolor. I imagine salmon and lake trout in the murkiness of the river swimming past invisible threads as they make their way to the freedom of the open waters of the lake just ahead.

This is not a place of picture-postcard beauty, but of character. There are no flower gardens, no sleek offices or elegant shops, just the steel and concrete of commerce. Yet here, so close to the urban center, there is sanctuary as holy as any unspoiled temple of green. Here, where gears of the city meet nature, there is peace.

John Fennell is editor of *Milwaukee Magazine*.

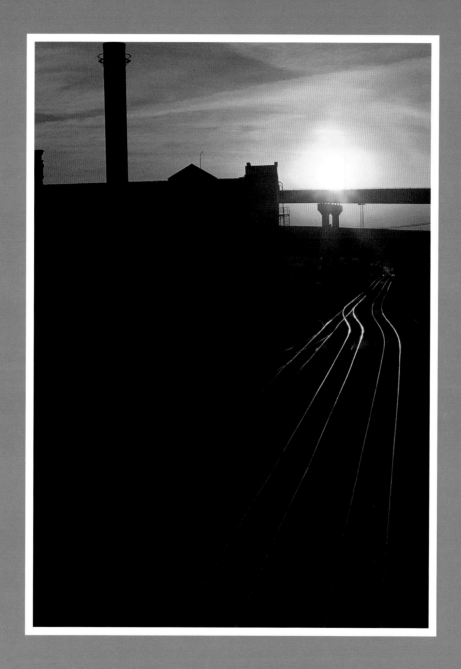

henry h. smith the low sun transforms the city's main train yard in the menomonee river valley

milwaukee morning

annette craig

rows of houses
   so close
that in early risings
   things
are seen and heard, not
meant to be, once outside
the cold that blisters motivates
two quarters inside my glove
   never warm
the bus in sight, an
ungainly monster
   eyes
too wide apart
   nose
too broad, we heave
and creak our way
over the viaduct
autos making their descent
down into the ravine where
thru the glass encircled with
   frost
I see railroads so tangled
as if a small child had
   scratched
them in sand, but their
silent switching reveals a
   plan
heady odor of malt and
chocolate saturates the air
as we move closer to the
tall ice-houses rising
in the sky, their furnaces
straining and tugging

fog over the lake, the
horn at the end of the reef
sounding the familiar
  "coo-coo"
the sky is white
  again
snow will fall and
  clothe
each branch and crevice
  with
a fit that is finer than
that of the choicest designer
it will freshen the tall
white slopes and undulating
drifts now in their permanent
  pose
till spring when
the same hand will
  rearrange
and decorate again.

Annette Craig has lived in four other states, has traveled coast to coast, but twice has returned to her home-town Milwaukee where she currently teaches music at South Division High School. Her work has been included in numerous publications, such as *The Hobo Jungle, Mind in Motion, American Poetry Annual*, and appeared in the *1996 Wisconsin Poets Calendar*. "Milwaukee Morning" was originally published in *Expresso Poetry: An Anthology by Poets from Audubon Court Books Expresso Bar* edited by Doris N. Gendelman (1994).

city reminiscences

hometown pastiche

helen padway

The names had juice in them
ss's and z's.
We did not know that they
would disappear like foam
in the glass—leaving
only the memory
of yeast and hops. A sweet sour
bouquet that drifted
over the bridges of our city.

In the valley the click clack
of Bingo chips drowns
the ghost of cattle sounds.
Now we have micro brews
and the roar of the Harley.
Rockwell International
displaced Allen Bradley
but the old clock glows
a four sided welcome.
Goldmans Department Store
with the slanted
wooden floor still lives
on Mitchell Street. Usingers
and Maders thrive
on Old World Third.

On hot summer nights we slept
at the lakefront a Michigan breeze
lifting tendrils of damp hair.
The pleasures of memory mingle
with the gains and losses of change.

Helen Padway lives and works in Milwaukee. Her poetry has appeared in many literary journals, including the *California State Quarterly* and the *Rockford Review*. She is also on the board of directors of Woodland Pattern, a non-profit literacy center and bookstore which tries to encourage and introduce writers and artists to the Greater Milwaukee community.

henry h. smith al's run, milwaukee lakefront,1989

c.j. hribal

I was in a bar with a friend when he turned to me and said, "You know what? Lately I've been feeling real sentimental about my wife." I knew just what he was talking about. If you're lucky, at a certain point in your marriage you've been through enough ups and downs that you know—know in a way you never knew when you both were simply young and glandular—that this really is who you're going to be with for as long as you're both alive. And you're glad.

What you get sentimental about are not the obvious things that first attracted you to each other. For example, the two dime-size indentations on my wife's lower back that flank her spine. I treasure these hollows in her skin. I am sentimental about them in the same way I'm sentimental about the shape of her nose or the screwed-up face she makes when one of our kids unconsciously says something howlingly funny. In the familiar there is intimacy, comfort and knowledge—the familiarity that breeds content.

Choosing where you live and being happy about it is a lot like being in the right marriage. You can simply feel it.

When my wife and I and another couple go out for dinner, we often take a stroll afterward—along the lakefront or in the Third Ward or up in the Riverwest neighborhood or maybe along the RiverWalk. Maybe it's the quality of light—the way it plays off of the buildings—maybe it's the good food, maybe it's I'm feeling generous and sentimental in middle age. Whatever the reason, invariably I will utter a good-natured sigh and say, "I love this town."

Our talk invariably turns to what it is we love about the city. Writ large, the answer is: It suits us. We trot out the usual reasons people like any medium-size city: not too big, not too small, good theater, good symphony, good public transportation, affordable housing, a good place for kids, et cetera.

Writ little, the love is in the details. Our respective neighborhoods—Cold Spring Park and Washington Heights—are both within a bottle cap toss of Miller and the original Harley Davidson plant. Our Arts and Crafts houses, our Heinz 57 varieties of neighbors, our churches, our kids' school—MPS, believe it or not. We like the convenience of having a commute time of nine minutes—by bicycle—to our jobs.

But it's more than just that. As with any union that lasts, there's the joy of the union itself. The little odd moments, the places and spaces that make you feel you belong.

If you've lived in the city for any length of time, you find yourself collecting and cherishing these moments. Discovering a secret route to the East Side that lets you sneak to the lakefront just an hour before sunset for the fireworks and gets you back home again before the traffic jams to the burbs have barely gotten under way. Coming home from the stadium with your kids on the day Sammy Sosa hits home runs 64 and 65 and everybody on the bus is buzzing about it, a public moment of shared joy and wonderment—"Didja see it? Didja? It was a-mazing!" Biking the Oak Leaf Trail on a Packers Sunday, the streets as empty as if a bomb had been detonated, and in the parks calling out to people, "Score?" and them shouting back happily, "10-3, second quarter." Rollerblading at dawn along the lakefront from the Art Museum to Bradford Beach and back, the sun a bright orange ball as it rises, the dark lake and the lightening sky telling you with every glide you take: Is it good to be alive in this town right now, right here or what?"

There's something else every good marriage has: discovery. I don't know everything about my spouse, nor do I want to. A marriage can get old in a hurry if you stop finding out things about each other. So, too, with Milwaukee. There are always delicious things to be discovered. There's always another neighborhood to check out—Piggsville or Concordia. Another neighborhood bar—the Uptowner or Harley's. There's always another gallery opening, another old building getting a new business or an old business getting a new address (think Miller Park). I walk, bike and drive down Milwaukee's streets with a constant sense of expectation, delight and glee. So much that's familiar, so much that's new, so much to feel a part of.

Marriage is, of course, one of humankind's most splendid fictions. Two people, through a miracle of will and desire, create a new entity. But it works because we believe in it. Marriages end not when love goes away but when belief does.

Call me old-fashioned. Call me a sentimentalist. For all of its faults—and Milwaukee has tons of them—I still believe. Milwaukee—I love this town.

C. J. Hribal is the author of *The Clouds In Memphis,* winner of the Associated Writing Program Award for Short Fiction. He is an associate professor of English at Marquette University.

the commute

brent goodman

My entire family has taken up residence in a depression-
era office building downtown and now roam the gray halls,

sleeping on wool couches, dreaming in low fog off the great lake.
Now they speak to each other through an elaborate network

of pneumatic tubes hidden behind the walls. Finally a place to catalog
the ghosts, handwritten lists, and a congress of stuffed chairs.

The most fragile inheritance: a thousand mirrored windows, my small
reflection in each. Tonight I approach the city through an interchange

of horn blast and brake light, the sun draining pink over coal barges
and mountains of salt. The air thickly sweet with hops and chocolate.

In the distance, the first silhouettes are already waving.

Brent Goodman is author of two limited edition chapbooks: *Trees are the Slowest Rivers* (Sarasota Poetry Theater Press, 1999) and *Wrong Horoscope,* winner of the 1999 Frank O'Hara Award. His work has also been nominated for a Pushcart Prize, and in 1998 he received an Individual Fellowship in Literature from the Wisconsin Arts Board.

roasting chestnuts

peggy hong

Sun setting in Dae-shin-dong
when mother slips her arm into
the crook of father's, to walk
down the hill to the grocery. Nerves
not yet damaged by disease, he skips
ahead on this night
that threatens frost.

My husband brings home a sack
of chestnuts from Glorioso's market
along with Genoa salami, mild
giardiniera, a pound
of locatelli. *Pahm*, Koreans
call chestnuts, the same word
as night, scooped into
brown paper bags from vendors
calling out along narrow streets
in Seoul, New York, Calabria.

I'll peel them,
I say, fingering the chestnuts,
glossy as my mother's once
unstreaked hair, if
you'll roast them.

He slits an X on each nut
and later, when they emerge
from the oven, I take one at a time
in my toughened winter hands, squeeze them
until they crack. I hear they all
come from China these days,
like my crocheted wedding dress,
this wooden bowl, a neighbor's adopted child.

After weeding out the green molded ones
we are left with exactly ten.
We share them, burning our eager tongues.

Back in Seoul, mother finally catches up
with father, at the corner next to a vendor.
He holds a roasted sweet potato
in one hand, an open bag
of chestnuts in the other. He waves
her over with the potato, and steam
escapes from his full mouth
when he calls out her name.

Peggy Hong is a poet who lives in Milwaukee with her three children and husband. She works at Woodland Pattern Book Center as education coordinator. She is the author of a chapbook of pregnancy and birth poems, *The Sister Who Swallows the Ocean* (CrowLadies, 1998). "Roasting Chestnuts" was originally published in *Bamboo Ridge*, No. 73 (Spring 1998).

outside the box

Reprinted from Milwaukee Magazine, 1997

stephen filmanowicz

Scents are what I notice first when I duck out the back door of my warehouse office building and ease onto Commission Row.

Even in the evening, when stains on the sidewalk are all that remain of the day's bustling produce trade, I can sometimes smell tomatoes, like moist earth seasoned with lemon. Even if I'm unlucky and catch the rot of bad potatoes in a dumpster, every walk here begins like spring—and reveals the winter in other places.

Like other people, I'm drawn lately to places that savvily bundle the things I like, places like Barnes & Noble, where Starbucks coffee, cherry wood and oceans of books act on my senses like one of those body-jet showers. But the powerful delivery system that attracts me is also what wears on me. The huge overhead at Barnes & Noble necessitates a big parking lot and a location on a high-bandwidth street that reminds me of how much I was carsick as a kid. If, as Robert Pirsig wrote in *Zen and the Art of Motorcycle Maintenance*, "driving is just more TV," then superstores are just more places to channel surf.

Downtown, by contrast, grows on me as I walk. It always takes a heavy snowfall or the first balmy day of spring to get me to ditch my car and head out from my office on foot, and then I wonder why I waited so long. The scents of Commission Row are just the first sign that I'm in a 360-degree world—a full-color Oz compared to the usual gray Kansas.

Most cars are far enough away to create a faint rumble as I pass Pfister doormen in their long coats. If it's evening, light twinkles in the trees on Jefferson Street and I feel mobile and untethered. I can stop in and see art at a shop called Eden, look for friends at Taylor's or just glide on home to the lower East Side.

At this pace, I find myself examining the city as a doctor would. The downtown streets, I see, are nourished by pedestrian red cells that make deposits and pick-ups along the way. With concern, I encounter some lonely, atrophied places—often spots like shops at Juneau Village that someone tried to revitalize by making more suburban.

Still, the health of the patient is deemed satisfactory. In an age when the multiplexes are all 15 miles away, it's reassuring to see a young couple in hiking boots slow down in front of a downtown storefront, reassuring to see that people choose to come here at all. Many of them know superstores and new "on-line worlds," yet they want more than these communities in a box. They want to amble and roam… and if they're lucky like me, get a whiff of tomatoes as refreshing as oxygen.

Steve Filmanowicz is a media and policy coordinator for the city of Milwaukee's Department of City Development. He is former senior editor of *Milwaukee Magazine.*

zane williams *madison skyline by dusk*

tim holte my city neighborhood

sunday at st. josaphat's

julie king

I suck on a host, a pearl freefloating
in a fleshy mollusk, waiting for birth.
I haven't taken communion for ten years
but remember the ritual, the thumb on my lip,
the satisfying chalkiness on the tongue.

When I was young, Grandma took me here
to sit in the Canski pew, fourth pew
from the altar, the claim the family staked
in basilica history, part of the Polish
immigrants' founding, ninety years ago.

But Canski is not my name anymore; I lost it
ten years ago to a rodeo cowboy. He took
me to Abilene, filled me with good whiskey
and babies, then sent me on my way
later when oil prices fell and line dancing waned.

I crawled back here, to the blood-sweetness
of Grandma's czarnina, bushas on Mitchell St.,
and the curse of boot-shaped noses,
one curse my babies somehow escaped,
giving Uncle Tadeusz suspicion.

But my family took me in, me and mine, rumbling
down National Ave. in a '76 rusted Bronco.
And as Father Pilarski raises his voice to climax
the closing prayer, the host finally dissolved
in ten years of bitter spit, I swallow, born again.

Julie King teaches at the UW-Parkside. She has just finished producing her first short film, "Worlds," and has published poetry and fiction, including a story in the Wisconsin Fiction issue of *Transactions*. "Sunday at St. Josaphat's" originally appeared in *Interim,* Spring/Summer, 1995, v. 14, n. 1, in a slightly different form.

the tin teepee

lynn shoemaker

Out the door and three steps down. Then my old-time friend and I set forth on the sidewalk, that concrete pet-roglyph from a time when the elders had strong hips. Across the street, my neighbor is vacuuming his lawn back to green. Jaw set, he marches back and forth with his leaf-sucking machine under his Packer flag. Halfway down the block, Mrs. Von Hoysen leans into Beethoven. Or is it boogie-woogie? Can't tell for sure, because the picture window sucks up the piano's notes. Almost always we hump through the park, cut by the pale stone war memo-rial, four-sided pillar, four wars, four bronze plaques. Once I saw a woman about my age, seated on the Vietnam side. Quiet, slow, she was staring her whole life back into that wall until there was nothing left except a young soldier's name.

Where is the wilderness, where is our wilderness, we ask. It's in our crossing over the wood plank walkway that crosses the University's wetland, home to that oldest of Earth's creatures, Mr. Buzz-Buzz himself, who will inherit the toxic swamp that our extinct species will leave behind. And God says to this mutating blood-prober, "survive." And it does. One glance at our new gas-fired power plant on the far northern horizon. They say it's clean. The sky walks right into its stacks, vents, burns its hair red, its body invisible. Then my friend and I make a quick pass through the downtown sector. Century Real Estate—too much business lately. Haney's Men's Wear—dressing you up for life. Dale's Bootery. Dale's Travel. Dale's Gift Shop. The Post Office. Novak's Café—home to mama's apple pie since 1937. Once we had an Amoco station. But the town bank kicked it out to the east side, rolled down an asphalt parking lot, complete with fake gold stripes. All these we pass by before reaching our one pausing place.

The old Carnegie Library, now the Chamber of Commerce, means nothing to the land. But out front abides our town fountain, a Neptune with four naked cherubs. Come November the city workers shut off the water and wrap our summer fantasies in a brown tin teepee. Feathers, drums, and Indian ponies—hokey designs painted all over it, some kids' initials too. I remember this year's Blue Mounds Powwow. Not very big, just a few dancers, only three contestants for the Miss Blue Mounds America Contest. Stubborn celebration of harvest, seasons, the plen-ty and the pain. I remember taking two or three intertribal turns myself, trying to follow the drumming, mostly stumbling and stubbing my big white toes. My friend and I stand here and stare our lives back into this tin mon-strosity. We do a little sashay dance. I turn to him and say, "This teepee is gonna stop the next war." He turns to me and answers, "Lord willin', son, Lord willin'."

Lynn Shoemaker was born in Wisconsin, but spent his childhood in Oregon and South Dakota. He now teaches in Whitewater, though he periodically travels to Central America on human rights missions and to California to see his doctor-dancer daughter.

zane williams fire drill, downtown fountain city

city culture

harley davidson's first factory courtesy of harley davidson motor company

the first harley-davidson motor company factory in milwaukee: universal icon for the city

dr. martin jack rosenblum

For many Harley-Davidson motorcycle riders—and those who simply enjoy the sound of one passing by—the First Factory that once stood in the City of Milwaukee has shaped the lives and dreams of countless people worldwide. When I first became interested in Harley-Davidsons as a kid in the '50s, I had imagined countless Harleys still rolling out of the First Factory onto the streets. I lived in Appleton, Wisconsin, and on my first visit to Milwaukee in the early '60s, going to where I knew the factory once stood was top of mind.

The fact that this building no longer exists makes it even more of a Milwaukee icon, for it remains on solid ground in the imaginations of those who have been shaped by its original presence. Today, as the historian for the Harley-Davidson Motor Company, I consistently hear from people requesting precise information about how this factory looked because they are either building their own versions, or have such a refined notion of it that additional facts are absolutely required.

The very first Harley-Davidson factory was built in 1903 in the back yard of the William C. Davidson family home. This residence was located on the southwest corner of what is now the intersection of 38th Street and Highland Boulevard. (The address was, at the time, 315 37th St.; the discrepancy relative to today's streets is explained by virtue of an official City of Milwaukee change of street names that took place in 1926.)

Before 1903, experimental work on building motorcycles was carried on at the home of a friend on Chambers Street in Milwaukee. After 1905, production of Harley-Davidson motorcycles took place at the current Juneau Avenue site, located still at 3700 W. Juneau Ave. Today, the entire site itself is listed on the National Registry of Historic Landmarks.

The original factory building is referred to in Harley-Davidson Motor Company literature as "the old shack," "a small (or 'humble' or 'modest') shed," "first building" and a "ramshackle little shop." All of these references are in contexts that take great care to portray that 315 37th St. backyard spot with reverence and modesty equally combined. To so many, there is no more famous landmark in the world.

What was the construct of the "old shack"? Keeping in mind that countless people have built replicas in their own back yards around the world, the nature of what that "ramshackle little shop" looked like is critical to Milwaukee history.

The woodshed factory was constructed by William C. Davidson, father of the three founding Davidson brothers (Arthur, Walter and William A.). William C. Davidson worked as a skilled cabinetmaker in the Milwaukee Road railway shops, building the comfortable and decorative passenger cars that were a signature of the Milwaukee Road passenger service. Given this professional background, and through a careful examination of extant photography of the first factory, it is not hard to determine that this so-called woodshed was by no means primitive; moreover, it was a sturdy building that survived well into the '70s when it was accidentally razed.

By all accounts, the first factory was 10-by-15 feet, measured on the outside. The front height was around 9 feet 10 inches, and the rear height approximately 10 feet 8 inches. It was of standard stick frame build. It had a shedding roof of a slight pitch, which was less than a rise of 2 inches for every 12 inches of run. The foundation more than likely consisted of squared timbers directly set upon the ground, on which the sill plate and floor joists, with 16-inch centers, were secured by nails. Flooring was probably set down in three layers. Due to the severity of Midwestern weather, the walls were likely also a three layer construction. Plain board sheathing was nailed to the 2-by-4 stud wall on 16-inch centers. One can surmise that there would have been waterproof paper on the walls over which the siding was nailed. Photographs suggest that the siding was white cedar strips, and exterior nail heads appear to be quite large, indicating 16-penny nails.

Door and window frames, drip caps, stops, fascia and corner boards were also white cedar. Lumber for door and window jams appear to be 2-by-6 inches, and windows were 6-pane units of wooden sash design. The roof was laid down with 2-by-6 inch standard rafters with a 4-inch projection running on all sides. Roofing material was heavy fiber or tar felt paper. Interior details can only be surmised.

Originally, the first factory was not planned as the site for a motorcycle manufacturing business. As stated by William H. Davidson, the retired president of the Harley-Davidson Motor Company, in 1990, "My grandfather was never in the motorcycle business, but the original factory was in effect his workshop. He built that original plant for this workshop, but it was taken over completely for motorcycle production."

When this now famous takeover occurred, the words "Harley-Davidson Motor Co." were painted on the door. This lettering was done by Janet May Davidson, sister of the three Davidson brothers. William S. Harley, the boy-hood chum of the Davidsons, was the one who came up with the engine design that was at the heart of the first Harley-Davidson motorcycle. Legend has it that the Davidsons put his name first on the door out of respect. The Davidsons were like that, modest and respectful. They were as humble as the first factory itself, out of which the Harley-Davidson motorcycles began to roll.

In fact, the first factory received a 3-by-15-foot addition immediately in 1904, just one year after production of motorcycles had begun, doubling the floor space! In 1905, another smaller addition was built. By 1906, a larger facility altogether had to be constructed on the site of the present-day Juneau Avenue building. And the first factory was put back into service for a time, too, to keep up with Harley-Davidson motorcycle production needs.

Around 1918, the four founders of the Harley-Davidson Motor Co., sensing historical value regarding the first factory, had the original 1903 woodshed section detached and moved to the Juneau Avenue factory site which had been expanded and completed in 1914 as it stands today. A plaque was created and affixed to the first factory, which read: First Home of Harley-Davidson Motor Co.

By the early '70s, the first factory had become somewhat dilapidated. Without permission or knowledge of then company president William H. Davidson, the original structure, on permanent display, was ordered to be destroyed by a plant engineer whose job it was to keep things in decent order on the Juneau Avenue factory site campus.

Some reports say that the first factory was ignorantly town down to clean up the grounds. Others say that it was inadvertently torn down because a building near it was ordered to be razed; confusion took place and both buildings wound up in a landfill that day. However, conceptualized by the faithful in a registry that is worldwide and in the mind's eye, that first factory has shaped a vision of Milwaukee. It exists in reality today more than any extant Milwaukee structure. It is a universal icon for the city.

In the late '70s I was in England, lecturing at the School of American Studies in Norwich. I called a cab to take me to my classroom from the bed-and-breakfast cottage where I was staying, and the cabbie asked me where in the States I was from. When I said that I was living in Milwaukee, Wisconsin, he quickly asked, "That's where that little Harley-Davidson factory is, right?"

In New York in the '90s, I took a wild cab ride from my hotel to the Bond Street Café where I was to do a personal appearance. I was on the road talking about Harley-Davidson culture and history, performing poetry and music related to the Harley-Davidson experience. The cab driver, when I commented appreciatively that he drove like a factory motorcycle racer, said that he had seen images of the first factory, and his buddy, a Harley rider, had built a replica of it in the patio area behind his house.

Thus, it is quite apparent that the first factory has shaped people's concepts of what Milwaukee is all about, defining the city in ways that create a mystique about it and the Harley-Davidson Motor Company. Milwaukee and Harley-Davidson are synonymous. Today we have a "Bar and Shield" (the Harley-Davidson Corporate logo) sculpture, replete with state and company flags blowing in the wind, kitty-corner from where the first factory once stood. On any given day, you can look out of our office windows to witness men and women standing contemplatively gazing at this series of brick buildings in awe and respect. Marriages are conducted here at Juneau Avenue.

This is all because of that first factory, and its permanent location—now in the hearts of those who know a lot or just a little about Milwaukee, Wisconsin—where the Harley-Davidson Motor Company began and still is headquartered. Though we have facilities worldwide, it is that humble little shed that signifies our existence forever. The first factory has never been in a better, safer place of permanent recognition than it is today.

Dr. Martin Jack Rosenblum is the historian for the Harley-Davidson Motor Company and is an established author and recording artist. Previous to his position at Harley-Davidson, he was associated with the University of Wisconsin-Milwaukee and the Milwaukee Institute of Art and Design. He lives in Shorewood, Wisconsin, with his wife and two daughters—and his Harley-Davidson motorcycle, which winters in the dining room.

zane williams the old 400 bar, madison

rudy's cornerstone bar and grill

dennis boyer

"Hey turn that polka music up once, wontcha?" came the loud request from the bleached blonde at the corner table. She rose a bit rockily on a game leg and pulled a stooped 80- year-old to his feet as a hostage to her dancing impulse.

Rudy simply shook his head, pushed a switch beneath the bar with one hand, and wiped the bar top with a rag in the other hand. He had seen it all before, before 1950, before he moved up from bartender to bar owner. He hadn't had a surprise in 50 years and hadn't uttered a cross word in that time.

"Mabel's not so bad," chuckled Rudy. "She was pretty, once upon a time. Had a pleasing personality in the days before men walked on the moon. Even had a nice smile up until the third husband."

He could have been talking about the neighborhood around his beloved Cornerstone bar. The small homes in neat rows sat squat on the north side of Paquette Street and the mile-long line of foundries, machine shops, and warehouses stood like weathered monuments on its south side. The grit and soot of the World War II boom had not yet washed away. All attempts at painting yielded the same garish results as Mabel's dye job. Both the neighborhood and Mabel had gone through a lot, but still had a lot of life left in them, though there was no question of either going back to the flower of youth.

So it was also within the four walls of Rudy's Cornerstone Bar and Grill. Years of tobacco smoke were a varnish on the wainscot ceiling. Signage for defunct breweries hung behind the bar like memorial plaques in cathedral alcoves. A collection of gallon jars with various pickled concoctions lined the back counter like specimens in a pathology laboratory. Racks of dusty bagged snacks dangled on wires suspended from the ceiling, the pork rinds and blind robins aged like fine wines. A trio of aged daytime regulars reposed down by the pay phone, where their teasing of female phone users provided the only break in their incremental embalming and mummification. Evidence of entropy was present, but only to the eye trained to detect subtle glacial movements.

Neighborhood sons and daughters who had left home for institutions of higher learning would sometimes return to Rudy's over the holidays. They treated it as a field trip and often brought fellow scholars and instructors along. Not, mind you, for the mere sociology of great uncles cussing in Polish and heated arguments over the best pitcher in the town's old industrial league. No, social sciences were only the tip of their iceberg. Distortions in the laws of physics and time prompted this casual academic interest. Returning offspring gleefully pointed out the many loops in the time-space continuum within Rudy's Cornerstone Bar and Grill.

The bar television would often blink off its cable sports shows and flicker into the dull black and white of commercials for 1954 Buicks and Texaco gasoline. There was a background buzz to Rudy's radio that always seemed to relay snippets from the shot heard 'round the world in the 1951 World Series. Overheard conversation suggested recent visits by Warren Spahn and Eddie Matthews. Murmurs of excitement and sadness focused on "news" of Sputnik, the Kennedy assassination, Vietnam, and the Apollo moon mission.

Those young visitors might have presented a paper on Rudy's at a phenomenological symposium if not for their tender feelings toward owner and patrons. Thus, only the whispered tones of conspiracy could be used to relay the secret withheld from the broader world: rail booze shot and short Pabst tap, $1, or Korbel or Wild Turkey shots with Blatz longneck, $2. This was the Grail itself to the thirsty who sought out the dusty tavern temple.

One might easily become a patron here based on economy alone. One might be drawn into Rudy's tight and sanctified circle based on the passions unleashed on Packer Sundays. One might share the profane liturgy of epithets hurled at the Bears and, for good measure, the Cubs and the White Sox. Or one might be content to wait patiently for one white-haired eminence of a retired machinist to cast his still measuring eye on you and calculate whether you are worthy to hear a tale of good family-supporting union jobs, vibrant community life in a neighborhood full of children, well-maintained parks, and air filled with European accents and the fragrances of mom-and-pop stores.

Archive, museum and temple sanctuary—the record and cadence of life past in one fair Wisconsin city is preserved at Rudy's Cornerstone Bar and Grill.

Dennis Boyer is a folklorist and author of *Great Wisconsin Taverns: 101 Distinctive Badger Bars.*

green bay's broadway

tom williams

When I first moved to Green Bay, few I met ever spoke of the city we called home. Eager to share how short a drive Madison, Milwaukee or Chicago was, gleeful to wax rhapsodic over Door County's sylvan majesty, none suggested a local bar or restaurant I just had to visit, few praised a specific street or neighborhood. In sum, it seemed that if I were to find out anything about this city by the bay, I'd have to investigate for myself.

Three years later, I think I can first attest to why such silence pervades about Green Bay. For one, it suffers the curious fate of being neither a small city or a big town. Yes, this is the small city that claims the world-renowned Packers, but it's also the big town whose checkout clerks cannot discern the differences between parsley and cilantro. A permanent identity crisis has settled over the land: Some folk want to maintain the quaintness of say, the pre-war '60s, while others want to drag Green Bay into the new millenium.

So, for an urbanite such as myself, the question becomes this: What's the citiest part of Green Bay? And my answer is: the Broadway District.

Now, if you've been to Green Bay during the past decade, you might read the previous sentence and envision me as one who equates "urban" with "squalor," who prefers his streets littered with flattened cans and rustling scraps of newspaper, or one who looks to the presence of prostitutes and stumbling drunks as the epitome of "character." As I write, Broadway still might leave a bad impression for the visitor. Many will only remember block upon block of adult bookstores, seedy bars and, in general, places where one doesn't want to travel when the sun goes down. But to walk away with this negative view means to ignore what is, in my opinion, best about our own Broadway.

For to my eyes, it displays one of any city's most provocative charms: the chameleon-like capacity to seem many things at once. Yes, the Dean frozen vegetable factory holds sway at the corner of Broadway and Dousman, but to its south is a wonderful Thai restaurant with a lunchtime buffet that's always crowded. And to its east is Titletown Brewing Company, the sort of urban oasis where one enjoys a freshly-brewed stout with fish and chips, meets friends, plays pool, and commemorates the end of the working week. So what do I see when I'm on Broadway? An urban space in progress.

Yes, it's a short drive to Madison or Milwaukee. Sure, the leaves in Door County are breathtakingly beautiful at this time of year. But why should I pull onto Highway 57 or I-43 when I can stay local with a trip to the Neville Museum for tours historic, cultural and artistic, then stroll over to the Hinterland Brewery for a pint of pale ale, and finally, fill my hand basket with rice noodles, fish sauce and heaps of cilantro at one of several Asian food stores? Why shouldn't I admire the inexpensive and wonderful handiwork on display at The Gift Itself or stop by for carnitas at Maria's, a coffee at Surroundings or Cup Of Joy? And in this brief itinerary, I've only scratched the surface.

Infusing Broadway's "makeover" is a civic association, "On Broadway," with grants and support for new merchants. The aforementioned new merchants—who offer anything from antiques to stringed instruments to facials

—are cropping up and bringing handsome facades to faded storefronts. The city too has chipped in with wider streets that haven't compromised the sidewalks overmuch.

Restaurants keep opening (and staying open), but venerable veterans such as the Blackstone Café—the spot in town for a late-night feed and bottomless cup of coffee—relocate and maintain their integrity. Asian and Latino immigrants are obviously injecting spice beyond cumin and thai peppers; their entrepreneurial skills should serve as a reminder to the folk of Green Bay and northeastern Wisconsin that a city grows beyond population as it welcomes new citizens.

Of course I cannot say that one will never espy a broken bottle in the gutter. And, yes, some oddities remain—the largest aquarium supply shop I've ever seen springs to mind—but in relief to these small tokens of "bad old" Broadway, one should see the progress that undoubtedly has been made here. And it seems as though upkeep and boosterism has not made Broadway sterile and dull.

For the life of me, I do not understand why city fathers think that to revitalize a downtown, a shopping mall is key. Our downtown east of the Fox River possesses a stark reminder of that mistaken belief. Though malls seem to be the places we increasingly occupy, there's no eclecticism, no verve, no funk or, to put it bluntly, no city, in those climate controlled chambers of consumerism and uniformity.

Broadway isn't for the Wal-Mart, McDonald's and mall crowd, but it is for the committed urbanite. It's a city street with budding vitality, the place where one might run into a friend and have an impromptu lunch or make new friends with the Hmong woman who sells fresh lemongrass. It's a city street where one can buy jazz, classical and punk CDs, new and used furniture, where one can people watch, where one can simply stroll. It is a treasure to cherish and sustain. Just be careful when you're walking there—it might change right before your eyes.

Tom Williams is an assistant professor of English at the University of Wisconsin-Green Bay. He is a 1999 recipient of a Wisconsin Arts Board Fellowship for Fiction. A native Ohioan, he is still adapting to life in the Badger State after almost four years here. His work has appeared in *American Book Review, Gulf Coast* and *Another Chicago Magazine*.

brady street: the continual traffic of subcultural chic

mary mcintyre

A sun-bleached blonde in an anorak and tie-dyed rainbow skirt. A leather-clad teenager donning an array of metal objects in the curve of one ear, his nose-ring bobbing in time with the stomp of his Doc Martens. A sleek, bobbed brunette wearing a black cocktail dress and blue ostrich skin boots accentuated with stones and quartz crystals. All members of the shifting parade passing by as you're waiting for the light to change.

Since the '60s, Milwaukee's Brady Street has become a microcosm of subcultural activity, establishing itself through time as a constantly evolving archetypal melting pot. Characterized by a kind of energy that brings forth a sense of the past, present and future, this street is known as a gathering place for exotic refugees as well as for those who may simply want to test their curiosity quotient.

My first Brady Street experience, in 1970, was inspired by a man who unwaveringly wore a crew cut throughout the 60's—my father. On a Saturday afternoon, I accompanied him on a visit to a new candle-making shop that had recently been opened by the children of a friend of his. Entering through the creaky, paint-chipped door and stepping across the old, unfinished floorboards, I recall being somewhat perplexed by his use of the word "new." After our drop-in, my father acquainted me with other shops located within hippie haven that featured many handcrafted items—leather goods, pottery, ceramics, jewelry, stained glass and yes, more candles. As we went from shop to shop, I sensed that he wanted me to be more profoundly impressed than I was.

I recall him saying, "Don't you see these people are doing wonderful things?" At the time, I was not acquainted with what was considered alternative or anti-establishment. At age 9, my idea of hip was watching "The Partridge Family," or ordering a hot pink happy face rug through an ad in the back of my *American Girl* magazine.

Growing up in the '70s meant wearing the right things, listening to the right music and seeking out the hippest scenes. The fall of 1976, I attended the Brady Street Festival at the insistence of a friend who was most emphatic about going since he'd heard that it may possibly be the last one (a rumor proven to be false since Brady Street continued holding their festivals through the early '80s). Having reached the East Side, required to park many blocks away, if we'd had any doubt as to where we needed to go, all we had to do was follow the herds of people walking in the same general direction.

Arriving at Brady and Farwell, we were met with a sea of sound and vision teeming with energy. I had hoped to take a look at the arts and crafts located curb-side, but quickly resigned myself to the fact that it would take too much effort to fight the swell of the crowd. We jimmied our way through the hordes to obtain our prized plastic cups of warm beer that we kept caringly clasped in our under-aged hands, and took in the sights that simply weren't to be found on the West Side. We spotted, among other things, a breath-taking bevy of androgynous creatures clearly inspired by David Bowie's "Ziggy and his Spiders from Mars." The crowd seemed to part for these iridescent, lacquered, body-stockinged aliens—glittering spectacles that glided by with seamless elegance, miraculously unmelting in the noonday sun.

In the mid-to-late '70s, the enthusiasm for Glam Rock we had witnessed on the street that day started giving way to an aesthetic of shocking severity that made one feel compelled to follow a strict unwritten code of rules. With the new decree of Punk and New Wave, my billowing blond Daltrey-like perm was hacked at the quick with just enough length remaining at the scalp to abuse with peroxide and experiment with henna. Bellbottoms were out. Straight legs were absolute. All Levi's 606s were switched out for 501s. The latest designer labels were to be shunned. Clogs and platforms were relegated to the back of the closet to make room for the militant march of spike heels.

More so than ever, clothing had become costume. I would scour the racks at the secondhand clothing boutiques located on Brady Street such as Orchid Annie's, Marlene's Touch of Class (currently located on Water Street) and, most frequently, Whiz Bang (formerly occupying the space of the now well-established Mimma's). These shops offered the best retro pool to draw from in my attempt to create a signature look. I purchased one floral-beaded cardigan after another along with coats of the '40s and '50s, handbags selected for their unique shapes and ornamentation, mixing and matching clothes of all eras—in various shades of black.

Much of my existence revolved around attempting to acquire precisely the right apparel to dress up in, and going out to rock unsteady in the cataclysmic scene of chaotic coiffure and leather jackets. The club I frequented most was Zak's (formerly located on North Avenue) to hear bands such as The Haskels, Buck Byron and the Little Seizures, Tense Experts or the X-Cleavers. Other clubs of the time were The Starship, Nico's and The Crystal Palace. Many nights at the clubs seemed like an amp-charged, highly cranked Romper Room in which you would consider yourself lucky to get home uninjured.

Exhausted by the edgy, amphetamine ambience of the clubs, every so often the austerity of slam dancing and beer spewing was abandoned to secretly take refuge in the true cardinal sin of the decade—DISCO. I would escape to The Baron (formerly located at St. Paul under the expressway) to bask in the vapor of designer colognes and surrender to the mechanized beat of The Village People, Sister Sledge and KC and the Sunshine Band. Submerged in electrified color of drag pageantry, I'd witness various incarnations of disco divas such as Diana Ross, Donna Summer and Grace Jones, who'd prowl back and forth flashing bleeding purple smiles, their heavily painted eyes transfixed like victims of some terrific spell.

The desire to brandish a new look or stake a claim to a secret hideaway will always be integral to the quest of self-discovery. Today when I go to Brady Street, I realize my sense of attitude has succumbed to a sense of nostalgia. This street serves as reference point for mythologizing our memories or observing signs of new scenes on the horizon, enabling us to recognize vestiges of our former selves. Drawn there time and again by its shifting, eclectic psychogeography, we continue to return to be part of a Polaroid that's never quite finished developing.

Mary McIntyre is a native Milwaukeean whose poetry, art and fiction have appeared in *Jazz Street* and *Dreams & Secrets: New Work by Milwaukee Writers*. Her latest work is a collection of fiction titled, *The Stone Playground*.

ned luhm brady street parade

the health department inspector watches her daytime talk shows

sue blaustein

In the window you see a lady fish curved upright
using her right fin to wield a two tined fork.
An apron around her waist, she shares the plate glass
with a woodcutter's wedge shaped rack of ribs.
Ricki Lake's show is on the black and white TV
on the card table at North Avenue Fish Market.
Boyfriend and girlfriend shrieking,
and boyfriend leans till his woven blue
What Would Jesus Do? car key necklace swings.
Today's inspection is a rerun of the one I did last fall.

Customers under the spell
of buffalo fish on ice
strain to hear what the fight's about today.

A 2 x 4 blocks A&J Liquor's rear exit; "White Teens
Who Dress Black" is on the screen. With orders
and clipboard, I join the owner by the register,
to watch the audience judge a white boy
in wide leg jeans. No one likes that his pants
ride so low. I review the codes about exits.
They start showing how the girls look; we coincide in feeling
that it's best you're only young once.

25 cent chips
bleed grease right through foil. Since November
they're 30 cents. The people find out
one bag at a time.

When I arrive at Love's One Stop, the same show
continues, on a set in the back room, out of sight.
The cashier wonders what's going on, so I tell her:
I saw pink girls with brown straight hair: braided Black girl tight.
At the front door of Bright Foods, dirt bikes trip me.
Cheese scraps on the slicer at Gold Star II. Abdel counts
the patient whole and half gallons and pays the Golden
Guernsey man. I catch Fox Six News at Noon while waiting.
About three excited minutes, or five. They promise to expose
new hidden dangers on the broadcast tonight at nine.

A rival says
"he ain't yours, you ugly bitch"
Kulwinder Lal, working
alone at Quick 'N Cash
watches Jerry Springer.

In the tavern basement there's company when the Beloit
Beverage man thumps down with a hand truck and the tie
wearing salesman from King Juice checks his company's
flavors and fruit flies patrol the bottom of the bottle chute.
Upstairs, Montel's guest says her second husband
is also her uncle. Retired men at Tiny's Lounge
only groan a little, as they too may have known
situations. "She don't meet too many people"
they analyze, then ignore the rest of her story.

Sue Blaustein is a food inspector for the Milwaukee Health Department, and an officer of AFSCME Local 1091. An excerpt of one of her poems has been selected for the public art installation in Milwaukee's Midwest Express Center.

matt nolen, artwork the social history of architecture

john michael kohler arts center, the arts & industry program

john mclean

The John Michael Kohler Arts Center is a 33-year-old, nationally acclaimed visual and performing arts complex, devoted to innovative explorations in contemporary American art. Its exhibitions focus on a wide range of concepts and directions, with particular emphasis on new genres, installation art, unconventional photography, the crafts, ongoing folk traditions and the work of self-taught artists. With the completion of its expansion, the new 90,000 square-foot Arts Center comprises ten galleries, an intimate theater, a flexible interdisciplinary performance space, studio classrooms, meeting spaces, six artist-commissioned restrooms, outdoor gardens and sculptures, the Flying Colors gift shop and the Carriage House Café.

Founded in 1974 by the Arts Center in collaboration with Kohler Company, the Arts/Industry Program is an ongoing collaboration between art and industry and remains unique among all American artist residency programs. Up to two dozen artists per year live on-site for 2- to 6-month stays in the pottery, foundry and enamel shops at Kohler Company. The artists in residence are able to produce entire bodies of work that would otherwise be impossible to execute in their own studios.

Sophisticated technologies, unlimited access to technical expertise, materials, equipment, studio space, housing, transportation, plus a weekly stipend create an unusually supportive atmosphere. Each year, another 12,000 adults and children get to witness this collaboration in action through factory tours, workshops and lectures by resident artists. Admission to the program is very competitive and is achieved by direct application by the artist, a rigorous screening process, and recommendations by peers. Major funding for this program is provided by Kohler Company and the National Endowment for the Arts. Recently, Ruth de Young Kohler was honored for the legendary work she has done to foster the careers of artists through the arts and industry program.

One of the most unusual aspects of the newly expanded Arts Center is the creation of six commissioned public restrooms, each by a different artist as part of the Arts Center's Arts/Industry program at Kohler Company. Because the Arts Center has fulfilled much of its mission through the years through first-hand involvement with artists, commissions and artist residencies, it was important that there be some involvement with artists in building a permanent place within the center. The washroom spaces provided the perfect opportunity to create permanent works of art in themselves that would not impinge upon any other space (see Matt Nolen's washroom designs on facing page). Additionally, it was decided to work with six artists who had not previously had the opportunity to create major public works. Five of them, Anne Agee, Yolande Macias McKay, Merrill Mason, Carter Kustera and Casey O'Connor, had previously been artists-in-residence in the Arts/Industry program. Matt Nolen came to the program for the first time to create his commission.

The Arts Center is located at 608 New York Avenue, Sheboygan, Wisconsin. For more information please visit, www.jmkac.org.

cities, past and present

colin kloecker 4th and Wisconsin

an alliance of cities

edward j. huck

Wisconsin cities truly reflect the diversity of culture, race and ethnic heritage that has made America great. Wherever you are in Wisconsin, there's a city nearby to add that special something to the quality of your life.

Watch the sun set over the Mississippi River from Riverside Park in La Crosse as the River City Jazz Band plays in the bandshell, then head down Third Street to sample the night life, or steer yourself toward a rack of righteous ribs at Piggy's on Front Street.

Inhale the aroma of roasted almonds at Milwaukee's Summerfest as headliner Jimmy Buffet entertains while the city's own Willy Porter performs on a side stage.

Watch liquid metal pour into a sand cast at a foundry in the Fox Valley or a Chevy Suburban roll off the assembly line at GM in Janesville.

Make a pilgrimage to Green Bay and squeeze into Lambeau Field with 60,000 other screaming Packers fans.

These are a few of the goings-on in Wisconsin cities today, cities shaped physically and culturally by laborers, artisans and mechanics who left their homes in the Old World or the crowded eastern states to seek a more free, more prosperous life. The vibrancy of our state today shows how well they succeeded.

Cities are where the economy happens. Wisconsin's industries are players in a global economy, as sensitive to the whims of consumers in Singapore as Sheboygan. But the international economic forces at play in Wisconsin today aren't awfully different from the forces that shaped the state's cities 150 years ago or more.

Although Wisconsin is best known as America's Dairyland, farming is not what made Wisconsin. The trappers came first, here to harvest the rich pelts of Wisconsin's abundant furbearers to satisfy the demands of fashion in the East and across the Atlantic. Soon, miners poured into southwestern Wisconsin to eke lead from the ground.

Commerce requires transportation, by both land and water. The mines first were linked to the ports of Milwaukee, Racine and Southport (now Kenosha) by "lead schooners," large ore wagons drawn by oxen. Then the Great Lakes and the Erie Canal tied Wisconsin to the eastern states and the world.

Agriculture developed around the mines, serving the miners and reducing the need for imports. Later, agriculture's needs for equipment spawned major industries for Wisconsin like Racine's J.I. Case and West Allis' Allis-Chalmers.

Superior, at the mouth of the St. Louis River, was settled in the 1850s but did not boom until iron ore was discovered in the Gogebic Range in 1883. In 1889, 900 ships visited Superior to take on and drop off goods and cargo. By 1900, Superior was the second largest city in Wisconsin.

It was lumber from Wisconsin that rebuilt Chicago after the great fire. The virgin northern forests have long since been cut over, but the forest products industry still sets the beat for northern Wisconsin's economy. Today the cities of Superior, Eau Claire, Ashland, Wausau, Wisconsin Rapids, Marshfield, Appleton, Neenah and Menasha still depend heavily on the forests of the North.

Ashland was a leading Lake Superior port for lumber, iron ore and quarried brownstone. Years ago, the area was home to 17 sawmills with three major railroads. Today Ashland remains a manufacturing center.

Eau Claire went from a one-sawmill town to a one-tire-factory town, but today it's in the midst of Wisconsin's Silicon Valley. Since 1992, property values have exploded.

La Crosse is a treasure. Surrounded by some of the most beautiful country in the world, La Crosse has created a quality of life second to none. The city's first lumber mill opened in 1852. By 1877, La Crosse was Wisconsin's second largest manufacturing community, building and exporting agricultural machinery and riverboats. At one time it had four breweries that produced more beer than any other Wisconsin city. Today La Crosse is home to the third largest University of Wisconsin campus and the summer training camp of the New Orleans Saints.

While Green Bay is best known for its Packers, the city was and still is a gateway to commerce for all of Wisconsin. Like Milwaukee, Racine and Kenosha, Green Bay provided industry and labor with a place to create their products and export them worldwide.

Green Bay's commerce is older than the United States—Jean Nicolet visited Green Bay in 1634, and Jesuit missionary Claude Jean Allouez established a mission nearby in 1673. Traders and trappers were not far behind. The region's history is highlighted at Heritage Hill State Park. Just north of De Pere, the park's exhibits capture the rich and colorful past of the Green Bay area.

Appleton, a city along the banks of the Fox River, is another one of the oldest settlements in Wisconsin. Lawrence College was chartered the year before Wisconsin became a state. Railroads multiplied in Appleton because of its location at the north end of Lake Winnebago. The first commercially successful electric streetcar line in the United States ran in Appleton. Appleton today remains a cultural and industrial center.

Oshkosh grew up at the spot where the Fox River empties into Lake Winnebago. A lumber town, the city rebuilt after fires in 1859, 1866, 1874 and 1875. Today it is known as the producer of trendy overalls and host of the Experimental Aircraft Association's annual AirVenture convention. The air show brings more than a half million aviation enthusiasts together every year, making Wittman Field the world's busiest airport for a few days, with traffic ranging from tiny homemade airplanes to World War II vintage B-29s and the Concorde.

Sturgeon Bay, Manitowoc, Superior, Algoma and Two Rivers were among Wisconsin's shipbuilding communities. Twenty-eight submarines were built in Manitowoc during World War II. Today, Manitowoc and Marinette continue a tradition of shipbuilding as old as the state. While Berger Boat concentrates on luxury yachts, sturdy Coast Guard cutters built in Marinette protect the waters of the nation.

Sheboygan, known for its bratwurst, today has evolved into one of the most beautiful cities on Lake Michigan. In the past a safe harbor for ships, Sheboygan has developed its lakefront into a playground for all those who enjoy Lake Michigan.

When the paper industry catches cold, central Wisconsin sneezes. But the area offers much more. Wausau and Stevens Point are home to major insurance companies. The Marshfield Clinic is a medical research facility with a unique rural mission. Wisconsin Rapids is in the center of both paper-making and millwork industries. Nestled against Rib Mountain, Wausau calls itself Arts Town, USA because of its commitment to the performing arts. Merrill is so American that both John F. Kennedy and Walter Mondale launched their presidential bids there.

On the Rock River, Janesville is a center for retail commerce and home of the last automobile production line in Wisconsin. At one time more than 160 companies manufactured autos in Wisconsin, including Chrysler, Hudson, Excalibur, Nash, Rambler, American Motors and J.I. Case. As home of the Beloit Brewers and many industries such as Frito-Lay and Hormel, Beloit is the gateway to Wisconsin from central Illinois.

The cities of Milwaukee, Waukesha, Ozaukee and Washington counties have become the economic power-houses for the State of Wisconsin. About one-third of the state's economic activity occurs in these counties. Cities such as West Bend and Waukesha provide great places to work and live.

Milwaukee, the state's largest city, influences the entire region. Milwaukee remains the cultural center of Wisconsin for music, theater and professional sports (other than football, of course).

Madison, the State Capitol, is known nationwide as one of America's best places to live. It's one thing about which *Money Magazine* certainly can't be wrong. With a low crime rate and the lowest unemployment rate in the country, Madison residents can only fine-tune their exceptional quality of life. And they do so through spirited civic debate, in some cases spanning generations.

After shortsighted city leaders rejected a Frank Lloyd Wright-designed lakefront civic center because they didn't approve of Wright's flamboyant lifestyle, Madison didn't give up. The city simply tossed the idea around for a few decades, dusted off the blueprints, turned the civic center into a convention center and built the thing. Now, as a private gift of $100 million endows a downtown arts district, Madison is challenging itself to improve its quality of life even more. It helps, of course, to have the twin towers—state government and the University of Wisconsin – providing economic ballast.

Although few will argue that Wisconsin's cities have their share of problems—they are the refuge of the down-and-out as well as the proving ground for the up-and-coming—they are also the answer to many. Wisconsin's cities provide us our workplaces and our playgrounds, the places where we live and learn. They are the repositories of our industrial might and our knowledge, and the places where much of life as we know it happens. They will continue to shape the future of our state as they shape those of us who call them home.

Ed Huck is the executive director of the Wisconsin Alliance of Cities.

sc johnson administration building, courtesy of sc johnson

the johnson wax administration building

kristin visser

In 1882, Samuel Curtis Johnson left an unsuccessful stationery store in Kenosha and moved to Racine to sell parquet flooring for the Racine Hardware Manufacturing Company. In 1886, he bought the flooring business from the hardware company. Soon after, he began selling a line of floor wax at the request of his customers, who often didn't know how to care for their flooring. By 1898, sales of wax, wood finishes and wood fillers exceeded flooring sales.

In 1906, Samuel brought his son Herbert Johnson, Sr., into the company as a partner, forming S.C. Johnson & Son. They expanded the product line to include brushes, varnishes, wood dyes and other new products, and in 1917 discontinued the sale of flooring to concentrate on floor waxes, car waxes and their growing line of home cleaning products.

The founding Johnson had a strong sense of civic duty, and both father and son looked to ways to improve employee working conditions. They shortened the workday from ten to eight hours, initiated paid vacations and profit sharing, and always looked for the latest in factory efficiency.

Herbert Johnson, Jr., took over the company on the death of his father in 1928, and even during the Depression managed to keep the company profitable through the introduction of new products. As the company grew, Johnson began to look for someone to design an office building to house clerical and administrative employees.

A local architect drew up plans for a typical Beaux Arts building, which company officers rejected as uninspired. Frank Lloyd Wright, whose career had been moribund since the mid-1920s, was suggested by one of the company's public relations consultants, who was familiar with Wright's work. Few others in the company had even heard of Wright.

Wright showed the Johnson officials drawings he had made five years earlier for a proposed newspaper plant in Salem, Oregon. The main room of the newspaper plant was two stories high, supported by thin mushroom-shaped columns that tapered from top to bottom. Mezzanine offices overlooked the printing presses on the ground floor. Johnson officials were impressed. Here was a design that would make the kind of statement about originality and creativity that the company wanted.

Wright promised Johnson that he could design an office building that would cost $200,000 to build. It would house 200 workers, offices for company executives, a conference room and a cafeteria. By the time the building was finished in 1939, the total cost, including the Wright-designed furnishings, exceeded $800,000. Some of the cost overrun was simply Wright's lack of experience with building costs—he had so few commissions in the 1930s that he hadn't kept up.

Wright tried to get Johnson to move the new company headquarters out into the country, away from Racine's south side industrial area near the factory, where land had already been purchased and cleared for construction. Johnson refused due to his strong commitment to the city and community of Racine.

Unable to convince Johnson to change sites, Wright designed a structure that created its own unique environment independent of its location. Wright believed the workplace should be as beautiful as a church, and as spiritually uplifting. (Wright wanted to install a pipe organ to give the workers suitable music to listen to while they worked. Johnson refused.)

Wright's design, one of the landmark buildings of 20th century architecture, is built of two layers of custom-made brick with cork insulation between. (Some of the brick was spirited away to use in the Jacobs House I, then being built in Madison on a very strict budget.) The building is circled by bands of Pyrex tubing, enhancing its aerodynamic, rounded feel. Wright's insistence on tubing caused tremendous problems because it was not until some years after the Administration Building was completed that a silicon caulk that would prevent leaks between the 43 miles of tubes was finally developed. To solve the leak problem, the company eventually replaced some tubes with sheets of corrugated glass, and in other cases covered the tubes with a protective sheet of glass.

The Great Workroom is one of the most famous interiors in the world. Supported by thin, tapering columns of concrete reinforced with a then-new kind of extra-strength steel mesh, the Pyrex tube skylights between the mushroom tops give a diffused light to the three-story-high space. The column design was so radical that the Wisconsin Industrial Commission would not grant a building permit until a prototype column was tested, since Commission engineers weren't sure the columns would hold the 12 tons that each had to bear. In the test, the column held 60 tons.

Surrounding the main floor of the workroom is a mezzanine, used for offices. The main building also houses a cafeteria, a theater, executive offices and a conference room. A second-floor arched walkway of Pyrex tubing joins the workroom to an annex that originally housed the legal and marketing departments, and a squash court. Beneath the annex is a large carport.

The Johnson Wax Administration Building (and the Jacobs House I in Madison) launched the nearly 70-year-old Wright, whom many had considered a sort of architectural elder statesman, on the second phase of his remarkable career. From 1936, until his death in 1959, Wright was constantly in demand.

The company and the city of Racine remain extremely proud of their building, and the company has made only those changes necessary to continue its efficiency.

Kristin Visser (1948-1998) was a writer and editor, and a student of architecture with a special interest in Frank Lloyd Wright. Long an employee of the Wisconsin Department of Natural Resources, she co-founded Prairie Oak Press in 1991 with her husband and partner, Jerry Minnich. Kris authored numerous articles in newspapers and magazines, and five books, including *Frank Lloyd Wright and the Prairie School in Wisconsin* and, with John Eifler, *Frank Lloyd Wright's Seth Peterson Cottage: Rescuing a Lost Masterwork.*

architectural treasures built of brownstone crown recall the boom times

claire duquette

A journey along Wisconsin's Lake Superior coast winds through communities built in the late 1800s boom times, when lumber was king, ships filled the harbors, and commercial fishing was a young industry. Most impressive reminders of these times are found in the magnificent brownstone buildings of Ashland, Washburn and Bayfield.

The rough red sandstone of the Chequamegon Bay was laid down beginning 1.1 billion years ago when the plates creating the mid-continent rift stopped their slow churning. Some 600 million years ago the sandstone settled, piling in layers forming what is known by geologists as the Jacobsville Formation, a band as much as 3,700 feet deep sweeping across the north coast of Wisconsin, forming the bedrock of the Apostle Islands.

The ancient rock has long been carved by glaciers, wind and waves, into the fantastic stone caves seen on Devil's and Sand islands, and on the mainland near Squaw Bay on the Bayfield Peninsula.

It should be no surprise this stunning rock, first carved by nature, had its turn carved by human hands as a prized building material. In the time when sheer muscle power carved the rock, not many could afford to build with brownstone. But with the advent of steam power, it was possible for work crews to efficiently cut and move huge brownstone blocks, and quarrying became a major industry in northern Wisconsin, with stones cut and hauled from quarries on Basswood, Hermit and Stockton islands, as well as near Washburn and Port Wing on the mainland.

Ironically, it was a Milwaukee courthouse built in the 1870s from a quarry on Basswood Island that gave Wisconsin brownstone its reputation—impressing builders with a pressure crush point of 5,426 pounds per square inch—over twice the crush point of sandstones form Maryland and England.

As the boom times of lumbering and shipping on Lake Superior grew, up sprang municipal buildings built from native brownstone.

Some of these treasured buildings have been destroyed—the Knight Hotel and old Ashland High School to name two. But many still stand, monuments to an era gone by when public buildings were considered a crowning achievement in a community rather than a plain, drab box housing workers. Many are on the National Register of Historic Places.

These buildings dazzle with their sheer beauty—built with arches, turrets, towers, carvings and pillars, they are architectural showpieces. But just as importantly, they are connections with history. Looking at the massive blocks, one thinks of the great-grandfathers working in the quarries of Frederick Prentice at Houghton Point, or the Superior Brownstone Quarry on Basswood Island.

Ashland, Bayfield and Washburn all hold brownstone treasures. There is the cherry red City Hall building, 601 West Main St. Built in 1892, it once housed the post office but now is a showpiece for the city, boasting a grand arched entranceway and a magnificent bell tower.

The Soo Line Depot Building, 400 Third Avenue West, was built to accommodate the train lines that burst through to Ashland in 1883, providing a new way to move lumber, grain and ore to Ashland's teaming docks. Trains move infrequently through Ashland now, and the once-booming central railyard no longer has any tracks. But the deep brown depot building still stands proudly, its massive lobby now separating two restaurants.

On the Ellis Avenue campus of Northland College stands Wheeler Hall, built in 1893 as part of Northland Academy. Wheeler Hall has always held classrooms, but while the proud exterior still stands, the insides were gutted and modern classrooms installed.

And on Lake Shore Drive, the spire of Our Lady of the Lake Catholic Church pierces the skyline, reaching heavenward in all its brownstone splendor. Traveling north from Ashland, the community of Washburn is more than blessed with brownstone monuments. It was the brownstone industry that helped build the city, itself established in 1883.

Many of the buildings on Highway 13 are trimmed with brownstone, but the main street prize is the Washburn Museum and Cultural Center, built in 1890 to house the Washburn Bank. The Bayfield County Courthouse at 117 East Fifth Street was built in 1894, when Washburn became the county seat. The stately brownstone pillars and huge dome bespeak the dignity of that time gone by. When Washburn was awarded $8,500 in 1904 by Andrew Carnegie to build a library, it was built of locally quarried brownstone. Sitting on a small elevation, the grand staircase to the library lets you know that this library houses something special. Further up Washington Avenue is the St. Louis Catholic Church, again, built of local brownstone.

In Bayfield, the old Bayfield County Courthouse, built in 1883 and now the headquarters of the Apostle Islands National Lakeshore, is another building once falling into disrepair that has been restored to reclaim its place as a proud public structure.

And anyone who has watched Bayfield draw close while approaching that tiny city from the Madeline Island ferry has seen Holy Family Catholic Church standing sentinel on the hillside. That place of worship, too, is built of the rock favored by the turn-of-the-century elite.

Yes, the wild brownstone cliffs, streaked and raw, are one of the wonders of Wisconsin's north coast. But warmed with a sunset, or standing still under a full moon, the man-made monuments of stone are in their own way no less wondrous.

Claire Duquette is editor of *The Daily Press*, published in Ashland, Wisconsin.

cities of the fox river valley

ellen kort

Over a million years ago, a vast shallow sea covered the central part of Wisconsin, including the entire Fox River Valley. Through a process of erosion and a heaving and settling of the earth, the land eventually rose above the water. The glaciers spread into the Green Bay region and gouged out channels of the Fox and Wolf rivers...This natural water route connecting the Mississippi and the St. Lawrence River basins would carry Indians, trappers, missionaries, and settlers to a land rich with promise. To know the Fox River is to know the history of this valley, for the river is the thread that weaves one generation to another in the tapestry of our Fox Cities heritage.

* * *

It seems that the Fox River has always flowed through the economic veins of the wooded region of northeastern Wisconsin that eventually would become the Fox Cities.

It was home to the Native Americans and to the early trappers and traders, a highway of commerce, the source of both supply and demand. Commerce first depended on it; the fur traders and early settlers would not have had business to conduct without it.

Then there were the people who came to push seeds into the rich soil that the river's watershed created, or to graze fat dairy cattle on the lush land. Theirs was the business of growing things, and for them the river was the primary link with the rest of the world.

The area grew, developing its own commerce, and the enterprising businessmen who came to the area quickly saw that the Fox had still more to offer. It had the muscle to power the region's early industry. It turned lumber mills, then flour mills, but perhaps most important, it turned paper mills, and paper making became central to the economy of the Fox Cities, forming a financial foundation that was almost unshakable, emerging virtually untouched by what had been hard economic times elsewhere.

The river also carried in its relentless flow another kind of power, something new and intriguing, and the youthful Fox Cities became the first place in the nation where a river was used to turn a hydroelectric generator and illuminate private homes. It was barely days after Thomas Edison put his first power company into business.

And thus the community that was to become the Fox Cities grew, building first on the economic footing of the river and then on its own strength.

* * *

And now ...it is more than economic prosperity that sets these communities apart from others. The difference lies in their extraordinarily high quality of life.

Appleton

Downtown Appleton has survived the economic challenge of additional retail centers in the suburban areas. In the Spring 1980 issue of *Lawrence Today*, William Brehm, Jr. (Director of Planning and Development, 1980) said, "A great amount of community pride and satisfaction in Appleton exists among its residents. A central theme is a pride in the downtown. There is an almost emotional love of College Avenue."

Music, dance, theatre and art are alive and well in Appleton. With its roots at Lawrence University, a population of 60,000 plus, and the largest city in the area, the city asserts itself as the cultural center of the Valley. School, university and college campuses provide concerts, lectures and film series.

From the strongly supported Fox Valley Symphony to the orchestras, jazz ensemble and concert groups at Lawrence; from children's choirs to barbershop and Sweet Adelines, much of the voice of the Valley is musical. And as much as its residents love music, they flock in even greater numbers to anything theatrical. The Lawrence Community Artist Series and the Lectures and Fine Arts Series of the University of Wisconsin-Fox Valley bring well-known performers and speakers to the area.

That Appletonians identify proudly with their landscape, their traditions and their mutual sense of community is evident in the hundreds of volunteers and thousands of people who line the streets for the annual Flag Day Parade (the only one of its kind in the nation), the Christmas Parade, and "Octoberfest"—when College Avenue is closed off to make room for ethnic food, craft booths, sound stages, bands and a variety of entertainment.

Kaukauna

Kaukauna, one of the oldest communities in the Valley, has also been called "The Friendly City" and "Electric City." The Fox River, with its 50-foot drop within the boundaries of the city, generates electrical power from five plants. Kaukauna's municipally-owned electric utility offers one of the lowest electrical rates in Wisconsin. Thilmany Pulp and Paper Company, a division of International Paper, is the largest employer and is nationally recognized for its packaging and paper specialty lines.

Revitalization of downtown Kaukauna began in 1980. A Downtown Improvement Committee was formed to work hand-in-hand with the East Central Wisconsin Regional Planning Commission. The '80s also brought a federal Community Development Block Grant for low-income and elderly housing, and new quarters for the Heart of the Valley Chamber of Commerce, which represents 13 communities from Appleton to DePere.

Downtown revitalization continues as one of Kaukauna's most important issues. Quoted while Mayor of Kaukauna, Robert Van De Hey said, "The people in this community feel good about themselves and you can sense the civic pride. You can walk down the street and talk to people and to the merchants and see it, hear it and feel it."

Neenah and Menasha

The League of Women Voters of Neenah-Menasha in the revised edition of *A Tale of Two Cities and Four Towns*, paints Neenah and Menasha as a "blend of town and country, a study in contrasts." Industries include both national and international giants in the fields of paper, printing, packaging and metal casting; yet ten minutes to the south or west is prime Wisconsin farmland, rich and productive. The waterways offer year-round recreational activities and beauty in all seasons, but they are working waters too, and historically have drawn industries rather than tourists.

Former Mayor Thom Ciske explained to the Northwestern newspaper: "The days of large department stores coming into a downtown and increasing shopper traffic are over. Major retailers now want the people there first. I think our first step should be to try to get office buildings downtown. When shopper traffic picks up because of this, then the businesses will come."

A 42-year-old mill worker who has lived in Menasha all his life explains, "We're kind of a small town with a personality as pleasing as a cool glass of beer. But people go other places to shop. Everything we've tried for downtown has failed. But we're used to fighting for what we believe in. We'll find a way to bring it back, just wait and see. Menasha won't die."

Neenah, with its dozens of decorative old Victorian homes, hundreds of sailboats in the harbor, the Bergstrom Art Center and Mahler Glass Museum, old clock tower and new auditorium, has a cultured look. Despite this seeming sophistication, Neenah is just as well known for its dozens of parks and its feeling of "hometown-ness."

Neenah came at their downtown redevelopment problem from a different angle. Viewed by some as a pioneering effort, The Future Neenah Committee (formed in 1982) is a mixture of private, public and political leaders, whose goal is to revitalize downtown by raising funds, involving downtown merchants and eliciting community support.

Neenah's first woman mayor, Marigen Carpenter, explained during her tenure, "More than ever before, we're realizing that the future of the city is in our own hands. With diminishing state and federal financial aids, the city must choose its own direction in the future and rely on its own resources. I've always felt that Neenah has a great deal going for it. The city is in sound financial condition, has a high quality of life, and potential for improvement."

* * *

So how do you best describe the Valley? Perhaps you start and end with the river where memories and tradition still cling like moss. Old Father Fox, a bit tired now, twists and winds his way through the very soul of the Valley. And for every mile, for every bend, there are legends and stories as old as the Grignon House, the Doty Cabin, the old weathered buildings that stand like sentinels in Appleton's industrial "flats." The Fox became a first highway, cradled and nurtured the early settlers and became one of the likeliest places in the world to build a paper mill. Few rivers anywhere have etched a more enduring history.

Maybe the Valley should be portrayed by its people. The people for whom the Fox became a handy waterway, who cherished a close bond, who learned to mesh their movement with the river's. The Indians, Jesuits and explorers. The fur traders, settlers and farmers. Today, the Valley has become home to Vietnamese and Hmong people from Laos with one of the largest concentrations of Hmong refugees in Wisconsin.

For all their individuality and differences, Fox Citians live and think in terms of "community." The common heritage of uniqueness and pride, stability and success give each village, each city, an insistent feeling that they, all together, are the Fox River Valley. This sense of community that has cast the shape of the Valley continues and is worth preserving.

Ellen Kort lives in Appleton, Wisconsin. She is the author of 11 books, including *The Fox Heritage: A History of Wisconsin's Fox Cities*, from which this essay was excerpted and six books of poetry. Her most recent book, *Wisconsin Women and Their Quilts*, will be available in Fall 2000.

zane williams main street, downtown edgerton

tracy will

The history of the city of Stoughton—two years longer than the history of the state of Wisconsin—shows the profound impact that geography, industry and luck have in the development of urban centers. An enterprising Yankee named Luke Stoughton came to the Wisconsin Territory in 1837 where the fledgling community of Janesville boasted several stores, a mill and William Janes' ferry service across the Rock River.

In 1846, Stoughton ventured 30 miles north and started building a dam on the Catfish River. By 1847, the dam was completed and his development began.

The community that grew up around Stoughton's lumber mill was first populated by Yankee settlers. Stoughton added a grist mill, vital to the growing community in the surrounding farmlands in 1850. As Norwegian immigrants arrived on the Koshkonong and Liberty Prairies, Stoughton's mill became the closest site for grinding wheat into flour. The arrival of the Milwaukee and Mississippi Railroad in 1853 cinched Stoughton's prominence in southeast Dane County. With its connection to Madison, Whitewater and Milwaukee, Stoughton gained prominence as a center for building supplies, farm equipment, commodities and wholesale and retail goods for farmers.

With thriving mills, a rail link, stagecoach traffic, a row of brick shops and hotels springing up on both sides of the river, and the old lead road passing through the center of town, Stoughton was Dane County's second largest community, eclipsing Blue Mounds. A bridge constructed over the Catfish River in 1854 replaced the footpath and wagon ford, and linked Stoughton's north and south sides. The south side was where wealth originated in the railyards, warehouses and mills that sprang up in cream brick and frame buildings over the next 60 years.

The Civil War introduced a young immigrant teen to the complicated task of wagon making that led to the creation of Stoughton's important Mandt Wagon Works. Too young to join the Wisconsin Volunteers 15th Regiment under Hans Christian Heg, Targe G. Mandt ran off at age 15 to work at a wagon factory in St. Joseph, Missouri. He returned at war's end in 1865 to apply his youthful vigor to building wagons. The factory founded by the young Norwegian immigrant became Dane County's largest employer through the 1890s, and became one of the nation's largest wagon manufacturers. Using goods, local materials and training skilled wagon builders, Mandt controlled freight wagon trade from Janesville to Portage. He added western agents to sell his durable, easy-pulling wagons as business boomed with American settlement west to the Dakotas, Montana and Wyoming. Mandt expanded every year after the late 1860s using capital from several Milwaukee investors. His success depended on producing good quality equipment that employed several safety features he patented, including safety rings to prevent runaway horse teams.

A nationwide depression from 1873 through 1876 hurt business, but Mandt prevailed when Milwaukee investors forgave much of his debt, pennies on the dollar. Business boomed until an 1883 fire destroyed much of the plant. Madison firefighters jumped a train to Stoughton when they received a telegraphed report of the fire, but their fire engine froze on the trip down and arrived useless and too late to stop the fire. The legendary drinking festivities following the fire drew harsh rebuke from the Madison newspapers and Madison's Mayor Conklin. The Stoughton

Fire Department organized the following year and purchased a coal-fired boiler in case similar winter fires threatened homes in their city.

Tobacco warehouses first rose near the rail lines in the 1870s. Edgerton dominated the local tobacco trade, but the large crops grown in Rutland allowed Stoughton to become an alternate storage location. With most men employed at the wagon works, grist mills, and planing mills, jobs came available sorting tobacco, and local women began to work instead of men. In the process, women trying to balance work and families inadvertently transformed a Norwegian custom into the great American institution known as the "coffee break" during the 1870s.

The first reported coffee break took place in 1871 at the former Greig Machine Company turned tobacco warehouse on Coffee Street. Women who worked for the warehouse owner Osmund Gunderson agreed to sort tobacco under the condition they be allowed to return home at scheduled breaks to have coffee, a snack and mind their children. Gunderson agreed to their conditions because he needed workers to fulfill the demand for tobacco. His tobacco warehouse supplied the cigar factories of Madison that wrapped more than a million cigars during the previous year. To improve productivity, Gunderson set up a stove in the warehouse so women could roast their own coffee and brew it at work, saving them a trip home and him lost work-time. Whether or not Gunderson succeeded in keeping Stoughton's working mothers on the job, the coffee break became an institution in workplaces everywhere.

Tobacco was good for Stoughton. What started out as a temporary plan to store and ship 25,000 pounds of tobacco in 1871 became a major tobacco warehouse complex that shipped three million pounds of tobacco in 1880. Tobacco buyers at first used available warehouse space, and demand created the need for eight new warehouses built in the last half of the 1880s. The peak winter season of buying tobacco from farmers, preparing and packing the leaf, and shipping it to local and national cigar factories offered employment for more than 300 men and women each winter.

Factory workers attending nearby taverns stoked the spirits of the local temperance movement, headed by Annie Warren. Her campaign against saloons, with the blessing of local religious and community leaders, became one of Dane County's most successful efforts to transform the habits of heavy-drinking factory workers and farmers. From the late 1890s until the victory of Prohibition, Annie Warren also rose to prominence in the Wisconsin Christian Temperance Union. It took until 1906, but their vigorous campaign to forbid sale of alcohol and close down the taverns achieved intermittent success. Wet and Dry factions alternately enforced then cancelled municipal "dry" laws with succeeding elections. Stoughton's local temperance ladies pressed their campaign regionally to McFarland, and south to Edgerton. Edgerton represented the temperance leader's perfect foil, a town with brothels and taverns, where tobacco was king, and regular train service offering easy entree to wets trapped in dry islands. The campaign to keep Stoughton dry also included regular forays across the Rock County border complete with temperance protests against Sunday liquor sales and service, white slavery and gambling.

Local groups battling fermented beverages also fostered several important organizations, including founding the city's Free Library in 1906. Aided by the Carnegie Foundation, it holds one of Dane County's best Norwegian materials archives. Stoughton's civic pride also expressed itself in construction of City Hall in 1905, and it was the only city in Dane County other than Madison to maintain and retain a hospital from its inception.

The politics of wet and dry aside, the Mandt Wagon, later the Stoughton Wagon Company, remained the primary employer until the World War I heyday crashed with the ascent of the automobile. From the turn of the 1920s and on into the Great Depression, the decline of horsedrawn agriculture emptied Stoughton of its industry. The city population of 3,431 at 1900 rose to 5,101 by 1920, then hovered between 4,497 to 4,833 by 1950. Tobacco-driven agriculture remained a constant asset to Stoughton, but the city floundered through the Depression.

The move to create industrial providers linked to automotive and gas-powered agricultural equipment was the impetus for the creation of Nelson Mufflers—which became Stoughton's leading industry between 1940 and 1960. The company got a fast start because of government demand during World War II. In 1952, U.S. Rubber located in Stoughton on the Mandt Wagon factory's former location attracted by southern Wisconsin's regional auto industry. Now called Uniroyal, the firm manufactured rubberized cloth for automobile and agricultural implement seat covers, and as of 1996 was the nation's only producer of "Naughahyde." Stoughton Trailers, another large industrial employer, manufactures semi-truck trailers for over-the-road freight haulers, perhaps in historical resonance with the Mandt wagon makers of the 19th Century.

The industrial growth and movement of commuters into suburban homes created a building boom in Stoughton that began in the 1970s when its population totaled around 6,000. In the year 2000, Stoughton was the fifth largest city in Dane County and home to more than 11,000 residents.

Tracy Will is a local author who wrote the *Compass American Guide, Wisconsin,* in 1993 (Third Edition in 2001). He will be hosting the weekly Wisconsin Public Television series, "Wisconsin Stories," beginning January 2001.

dasengelflugenhaus—the history of a home

randolph d. brandt

Wilkommen to DasEngelflugenhaus.

Though the "haus" is more than 70 years old, its name is of extremely recent vintage. Indeed, my wife and I settled upon the name in the Spring of 1999 when, among my many move-in chores, I happened to replace a burned-out frosted light bulb over the front door with a crystal-clear variety. The light pattern from the electric lantern formed a distinct pair of angel's wings. Thus, Bonnie and I invented our own German word name for the home, translated directly as "The Angel Wing House."

It may be the first formal name for the place, a rather modest brick, story-and-a-half home on the north end of Racine. Though distinctive for a variety of reasons, the house really isn't all that much of a standout in a historic community known for its variety of true architectural treasures. Even a new fancy moniker probably won't qualify our house for Preservation Racine's annual tour of historic homes anytime soon. There are many more interesting and worthy homes available to study and appreciate in our adopted Sesquicentennial town. Still, unraveling the story of one early 20th-century home told us much about how Racine developed in its post-formative expansion years. We purchased the house at 3429 N. Main Street. on April 15, 1999, but the history of the land obviously goes back much, much further.

We know that long, long ago Indians were here. Though there's no apparent physical evidence of Native American occupation left in our immediate neighborhood, it is known that Racine once was inhabited by mound builders of the Hopewell Culture. Later, it was the territory of the Miami. In the decades before occupation by French, then English settlers to the region, the Potawatami lived around here. Their villages stretched along the western shore of Lake Michigan, destined to be displaced by the European trappers and traders and, eventually, farmers from Europe who would claim the land as their own.

In the middle of the 19th century, such farmers included many Austrian and German immigrants with names like Kasper, Reichert and Kupper – folks who'd know right off what DasEngelflugenhaus meant, if they still lived in the neighborhood. One such farmer was Michael Kupper, who came to Wisconsin in 1852 and managed to acquire 25 acres about a mile north of Racine in what was then part of Caledonia. It would appear from old plats of the section that our property once was a small corner of Herr Kupper's farm. Here, Kupper and his wife, Susan, raised two girls and two boys, presumably along with a little wheat, perhaps some produce and animals.

It would take decades for residential development to spread this far northward from town, but Racine expanded over time, with annexations creeping closer to the Kupper farm. The countryside out beyond the brickyards that existed where the Racine Zoo is now remained mostly in farm fields or grasslands into the early part of the 20th century; it was probably never thickly forested. It wasn't the best soil for growing crops either, which might help explain the current sorry state of our roses. A relatively thin layer of topsoil gives way quickly to the clay and sand left over from the old lakebed. That worked out well for the brick makers, though.

Brickyards and kilns dotted the lakeshore north from Racine to Wind Point into the 20th century, firing the light-colored cream brick used to build many of Racine's more historic houses.

In the boom years of the 1920s, large tracts of farm fields and meadows north of town gave way to land investors and their surveyors. Groups of Racine businessmen and real estate speculators, including descendants of the pioneer Miller family, filed plats for the first suburban residential subdivisions this far north of town. By 1928, the property was part of the estate of the late William Henry Miller, son of early Racine resident Moses Miller. Executors transferred the land to John D. Costello. Costello, who later would serve as Racine's postmaster, subdivided a portion of the property into the Lakecrest Addition.

It was a heady time for land investment, with large-scale real estate development riding the crest of prosperity and continued high expectations. Few would have reason to suspect that a looming stock market crash the following year would touch off the Great Depression. Meanwhile, the city of Racine continued to expand. The northern boundary of the city was extended again, annexing tracts to the border of what would become North Bay.

Getting in on the ground floor was Elmer F. Bornofska, a projectionist for the downtown Palace Theater. Bornofska and his wife built their home on the center lot, one of the first houses in the new suburban subdivision carved out of the farm fields along North Main Street. But shortly after their roof went up, the roof fell in on the nation's economy and as a result, one of the first houses in the new subdivision would stand isolated for years, at the city's northern boundary. Economic contractions of the 1930s would have a severe impact on plans for residential development throughout the country. Housing starts fell by nearly 90 percent nationally, and except for mansions along Lake Michigan, development of residential housing in north Racine was similarly affected. Many lots in the new northern subdivisions remained unsold for years. One tract several blocks away was used for a time as a "city garden," where residents could plant, grow and harvest their own food to help survive in Depression times.

Bornofska didn't survive as a homeowner, and he surrendered the house and remaining land to the bank in 1935. The house was rented in the interim by Frank J. Wemmert, president of Service Printing Company in Racine, and his wife, Florence. His grand-nephew, John Wemmert, recalls visiting the home as a young teen, roaming the still open meadows to the north and going to the nearby Lake Michigan beach with his great aunt. As better times returned, the house was sold to Emilie and George D. McLaughlin, director of laboratory research for BD Eisendrath Tanning Company, who began reassembling the original Bornofska parcel and expanding the house.

The neighborhood expanded too. The postwar building boom eventually filled in most of the lots along the residential streets, platted as far back as 1928. Creation of the suburban village of North Bay immediately north of Racine cut off further annexations for the city in the 1950s. Still, it wasn't until the early 1990s that the final open meadows in the area were carved into modern cul-de-sacs for new upscale housing. After World War II, the house and the lot were acquired by Thomas A. Laffey and his wife, Mildred. City directories list Laffey alternately as a foreman and superintendent for Western Printing Company in Racine.

In 1971, the house was sold to John O. Gerlach, president of Midland Container in Franksville, and his wife, Lorraine, then a kindergarten teacher at Roosevelt School. The Gerlachs loved the home, hosting dinners for friends and an annual end-of-the-school-year juice-and-cookie picnic in the back yard for Lorraine Gerlach's kindergartners. Early in the 1970s, the row of maple trees that line the property along North Main Street were threatened with removal by the city, which claimed the trees were diseased and had to be cut down. John Gerlach protested the decision, guarding the trees personally for an entire day to block their destruction. His efforts paid off. The large, old trees remain, providing a shaded front yard and an attractive arch over the eastern side of the street.

We acquired the home in the late 1990s when I relocated to Racine from the Seattle area to become editor of the local newspaper, *The Journal Times*. We are building our own memories here, and perhaps leaving our own lasting touches on the house and the landscape to survive us. In this new millennium, we pledge to try to be good caretakers of the house and the land, worthy successors to those who came before us and, hopefully, responsible stewards of the blessings of place for the next folks who'll come along.

Randolph D. Brandt is a fourth-generation journalist, part of a family legacy that dates back nearly 150 years. He and his wife, Bonnie J. Hollis (also a journalist and editor), moved from Seattle to Racine where he works as editor of the *Racine Journal Times*.

brent nicastro a winter view of madison's marquette neighborhood

the role of cities

tom bamberger looking north from bay view

the wealth of cities—the milwaukee advantage

mayor john o. norquist

George Kennan, foreign-policy scholar and former ambassador to the Soviet Union and Yugoslavia, was born and raised in Milwaukee. In 1990, he returned to receive an honorary degree from the University of Wisconsin-Milwaukee.

Kennan arrived a day early to tour his hometown, which he had not seen for 40 years. As mayor, I accompanied him. We visited various landmarks and fondly remembered sites from Kennan's youth. Although some were gone, he delighted in those remaining. We ended our tour at one of Kennan's favorite boyhood spots—a small downtown park.

In Kennan's youth, train stations abutted the park on three sides: the Milwaukee Electric Railway; Milwaukee Union Station, proud home of "The Hiawatha"; and North Shore Railway, the one-hundred-mile-per-hour electric train that connected Milwaukee to Chicago in only 70 minutes. In those days, when young Kennan finished his paper route, he would bike to the park if he had extra papers. To him, the park seemed like the center of the world, with thousands of passengers coming and going. It was a simple city park, grass and trees surrounded by buildings full of human activity, making its little green common all the more valuable. Kennan would sell his papers, all of them, fast, and he had great fun doing so among the excitement and crowds generated by the nearby trains, hotels, restaurants, offices, shoeshine stands and saloons.

That day in 1990, Kennan stood in what is now called Zeidler Park and his eyes moistened. All three train stations were gone. The park was empty and quiet. The only sound was the roar of the freeway a block away. Kennan looked off toward a concrete parking ramp. He shook his head and said, "This is not an improvement."

Economic decline in American cities began with the Depression, but it accelerated after World War II. Federal programs supposedly intended to help actually drained cities of vitality.

The suburban edges of U.S. cities have been encouraged to prosper for the past 50 years, while the centers have been allowed to emulsify. First came segregated suburban housing, developed with Federal Housing Administration subsidies. Then came heavily subsidized interstate highways to service the commuter communities; then retail shopping malls; and eventually, the whole workplace itself moved to the suburbs as office parks. Throughout Wisconsin and the U.S., the disassembled ingredients of the city sprawled across the suburban landscape, creating a situation where people travel further and further between increasingly insignificant destinations.

People, places and products are the ingredients that, when blended together in a city, generate wealth and, in turn, culture and religion.

Nothing could be better calculated to destroy this recipe than the current U.S transportation policy. Since 1957, when Congress passed and President Eisenhower signed the Interstate Highway Act, the federal government has spent trillions of dollars on multilane freeways that slice through complex networks of urban avenues, boulevards, streets and alleys like chainsaws. People, products and places sit stranded and strangled by freeways—the very ties intended to bind. Freeways have extracted homes and businesses from cities and dispersed millions of U.S.

citizens and businesses to the suburbs and beyond. Classic urban transportation systems, including rail, street-cars and trolleybuses, once privately financed and operated, have been undermined by the federally subsidized intrusion of freeways.

These new roads have left in their wake vast wastelands in New York's South Bronx, Cleveland's West Side, Cincinnati's West End, and countless other cities, some of which are just now struggling to regain some degree of vitality. Then there's Detroit, where every freeway ever planned was built.

My parents honeymooned in Detroit in 1946, guests of a grateful government that provided a week in a hotel to those who were POWs during World War II. My parents could choose between Minneapolis and Detroit. Since they lived in St. Paul, Minnesota, they chose Detroit.

They stayed at the luxurious Book Cadillac Hotel. With a new Bell and Howell movie camera, my father recorded the first days of an enduring marriage and the heyday of downtown Detroit. At that time, Detroit bustled with pedestrians and shoppers in scenes reminiscent of the great cities of Europe. Three department stores—Hudsons, Kerns and Crowleys—all on Cadillac Square, rivaled Manhattan's Bloomingdale's, Macy's and Gimbels. Detroit's prominent skyline was surpassed only by those of Chicago and New York.

Fifty years later, Detroit has changed beyond recognition. The pedestrians are gone. The streetcars are gone. The department stores are gone. Most buildings are gone or boarded up. The 28-story Book Cadillac, now pad-locked, has joined the Detroit acropolis of empty skyscrapers.

If money is the measure, the federal government kept faith with Detroit during its decline. But if results matter, Washington's dollars were fool's gold. Billions flowed from Washington into Detroit in the form of concrete—freeways that dismayed George Kennan in Milwaukee. Billions more built public housing in the city and tax-subsidized middle-class housing in the suburbs. More was spent on urban renewal and parking lots—so many parking lots that there are not many places left to visit.

I disagree, though, with urban doomsayers that say our cities are dead or dying. Despite the stigma attached to cities and the drive to suburbanize, cities still have charms and advantages not matched in suburbia. It is true that cities have been damaged, but they are far from terminal.

In fact, cities have some natural advantages that could allow them to lead an economic and cultural renaissance. Their physical properties—scale, proximity and diversity—are their chief advantages. The benefits that accrue where large numbers of diverse people live and work closely together include the most efficient results in transportation, labor exchange, consumption, capital allocation, culture and education.

One of the most striking physical advantages cities hold is their physical form. For example, in almost any metropolitan area in the country, the local news begins with an aerial view of the downtown skyline. Why? Because the downtown is the most striking visual aspect of a city. Imagine starting the news each night with an image of a suburban strip mall and its parking lot. The downtown provides focus and context and helps define the metropolitan community. Celebrations, charity races, parades and festivals—incongruous in malls or edge cities—are usually held downtown.

These images and landmarks are often depicted on postcards. Cable cars, the Statue of Liberty, the Eiffel Tower, the Wrigley Building instantly identify their respective cities.

I use slides to illustrate a speech I often give on urban design. The show juxtaposes slides of traditional urban design with slides of suburban sprawl.

"Would you put this on a postcard?" I ask my audience. "If the answer is no," I caution, "why build it that way?" When people view direct comparisons of traditional urban design with sprawl, they inevitably prefer the traditional forms. What repels is the giant parking lots positioned in front of buildings, the pylon signs, the lack of sidewalks, the disorienting jumble that constitutes much of postwar suburban style. And yet, almost everything new is built as sprawl.

Why? It's not only because of the market or consumer preference. It is because post-war zoning and planning require sprawl by law, and because state and federal housing and transportation programs subsidize it.

Unlike sprawl, traditional neighborhoods concentrate population and utilize public space in the most pleasing way. And these neighborhoods have simple features—sidewalks, houses with porches, main streets—that reinforce a sense of community missing from most sprawl developments.

Perhaps the most lamentable feature of sprawl is the disappearance of the sidewalk. Here's what *American Enterprise* editor-in-chief Karl Zinsmeister has to say:

> *A sidewalk gives you the permission, and opportunity, to place yourself pretty close to other people in their most intimate sanctums—their yards and gardens, their front parlors, the stoops and porches where they read their newspapers on warm evenings. ... A neighborhood where all the homes are laced together by an open footpath is a very different place than a neighborhood of houses reached only by private driveways.*

Public and private lives can gracefully mingle on our front porches. We are at home sitting on a front porch, with all its attendant benefits, including a modicum of privacy, yet we are simultaneously offering ourselves as a participant, passive or active by choice, in the public scene. We can quietly observe passersby as well as other porch sitters, or we can wave at them, or call to them, or invite them over, or ignore them altogether. On the porch, the option is ours.

Most traditional urban homes have front porches. Homes in cul-de-sac suburbia typically don't. They may have concrete stoops where a person can sit, waiting for someone to drive up and stick a newspaper in the tube at the end of the driveway. They may have ornamental imitations of front porches that are not even deep enough for people to sit down without bumping their knees. But they don't have real porches.

One reason for the small number of front porches in cul-de-sac suburbia is that there's nothing to see from them except lawns and garage doors. There are no children playing on the sidewalks because there are no sidewalks. There are a few joggers, walkers, or bicyclists passing by, but there is no community life in which residents can participate simply by seeing or being seen. People enjoy this privacy, but they can feel alone. They fear strangers, but they miss the community of friends, acquaintances and other citizens.

Another element of traditional neighborhoods is the main street. An excellent example of a main street is Kinnickinnic Avenue in Milwaukee, which extends through Milwaukee's close-knit Bay View neighborhood. Old maps of Milwaukee show Kinnickinnic Avenue, locally known as "KK," as one of the first routes to the city from the south. Eventually a double-track streetcar was laid along the avenue. As the area became urbanized, city engineers established a street-grid system that encompassed "KK and its local lanes and byways. By the turn of the century, KK had become the downtown of Bay View, lined with shops, offices and apartments.

On KK, the family-owned businesses are doing well. There are almost no vacant storefronts. Crime is rare along KK. The Bayview Library on KK is among the most popular in the city. The neighborhood is a clean and friendly place.

KK's design is traditional, graceful and simple. It is 50 feet wide, bordered by eight-foot sidewalks. Streets aren't built like that anymore, but until 40 years ago, 50 feet, or two-rods, was a common width for a commercial street. And it works well. A lane-and-a-half of traffic can move in either direction, cars can park on the street, and motorists have enough room to slip around double-parked cars. KK is wide enough to allow for traffic flow, narrow enough to encourage pedestrian crossings. The buildings that face each other across a 50-foot street aren't spatially or architecturally divorced from one another. They work together across that span to create a connection.

The shops along KK abut the sidewalks. There is no building setback. Motorists don't need pylon signs to identify the establishments along KK. They can look at the signs on the buildings or right in the shop windows and see for themselves.

And motorists have time to look. They are neither rocketing past at 50 miles per hour, nor riding the brake and checking mirrors in bumper-to-bumper traffic. Traffic moves smoothly even at rush hour. KK has short blocks and is nestled in a convenient grid. If the street congests, motorists can easily switch to a parallel route a few blocks away.

KK is a pleasant place to walk too. Your destination may be the hardware store, but on the way you just might take the time to stick your head in the door and say hello at Pankow's barbershop or catch a cold beer at 100-year-old Kneisler's White House tavern.

Most buildings along KK are simple, with retail on the first floor and apartments above. Some, like Kneisler's, are spectacular, but most are modest. There are brightly painted, flat-roofed clapboard affairs, or feature Victorian embellishments; still others have adopted the Milwaukee bungalow style. Together these buildings create a street that still reflects much of the scale and character of its 19th century village origins. At well over 100 years old and counting, Kinnickinnic Avenue holds its value and adds it to the rest of the city.

Main Street is not a sole Milwaukee trait. Like KK, Cedarburg's main street is 50 feet wide with sidewalks on each side. Buildings relate to each other in a way that creates destinations and community. Its specialty shops and other commercial enterprises attract shoppers all year long.

Since World War II, Main Street has been newly constructed in very few places; two of those places are Disneyland and Disneyworld. Walt Disney understood, perhaps better than anyone else, the charm of traditional urban America. When you walk through the front gate of Disneyworld, you don't see a strip mall. You see Main Street. Buildings conform strictly in line. Retail shops occupy the street level, and replica apartments or offices are above. Wide sidewalks accommodate pedestrians who enjoy browsing along the big shop windows. The street is a near-exact replica of the two-rod street.

Nostalgia is only part of Disney's popularity. People realize, on some level, that traditional forms work. And that's what is important for cities—not hailing back to some amber-hued days, but resurrecting what works. It works in Cedarburg and in Milwaukee's urban village on Kinnickinnic Avenue, just like it works in Greenwich Village, New York, and thousands of downtowns, small towns and urban neighborhoods around the country. Visitors to Disneyworld would do well to remember this. They just might find what they are looking for if they search a little closer to home.

George Kennan's boyhood urban paradise, though damaged, still exists all over Wisconsin. Our state is a great place for urban life, whether it's Milwaukee, Madison, Kiel, Cedarburg, or Port Washington, because most of our small cities and towns retain the basics of traditional urban living—sidewalks, front porches and main streets.

The community that so many Americans seek in the fantasies of Disney actually exists in the main streets of Wisconsin. The only difference is that in Port Washington, you don't need to pay admission. The beauty of Main Street is still available in cities throughout Wisconsin. After 50 years of sprawl caused by bad transportation policies and bad planning and zoning, it's time to save the places we love and build new places that can be loved even more.

John O. Norquist is the 37th Mayor of Milwaukee and co-founder of New Urbanism—a land use reform movement that seeks to recreate the density, diversity and pedestrian orientation of traditional neighborhoods. Mayor Norquist is a prominent participant in national discussions of urban design and educational issues. His book, *The Wealth of Cities,* focuses on federal and state policies that have contributed to sprawl and urban decline and offers a wide array of strategies to sustain urban vitality.

why do we need milwaukee?

Reprinted from Milwaukee Magazine, June 1995

bruce murphy and tom bamberger

Editor's note: Although the authors of this article were investigating the role of the City of Milwaukee, similar questions could and have been asked about cities in general. Why do we need cities? Perhaps some of the answers below shed light on that larger question as well.

"The city is doomed," Henry Ford once declared, foreseeing the impact of his mass-produced car on the landscape of America. Within decades, as the flight to the suburbs accelerated, his prediction seemed to be coming true. The great suburban migration created a new class of villages with the power to elect presidents.

In Milwaukee, though, suburbanization came slower. Even as late as the 1950s, the city was where you'd find the best stores and restaurants, where there were more and better roads and hospitals and playgrounds.

But in the Milwaukee of 1999, the suburbs have clearly won the battle of location, location, location. Drive through Washington County or Ozaukee County and you're in the land of excavations, with new homes popping up everywhere.

In the heyday of Milwaukee, factories had to be located in the city to be close to water and rail transport and other industries. Cities were the engines of economic development, the place to go to get ahead. People moved here from rural areas seeking better schools and jobs. Cities were the place to shop, eat, be seen and be merry.

Today, a suburban mall like Mayfair does more business than Grand Avenue. With the advent of car phones, faxes and computers, businesses can seemingly locate anywhere and many people work out of their suburban homes. The best jobs are created outside the city, and Milwaukee needs a residency requirement to keep its public employees from fleeing to the suburbs.

Today, we tend to define cities more by their lack of merriment. Phrases like the misery index, hypersegregation and drive-by shootings automatically come to mind. Growing economic and racial isolation threaten to replace the city's traditional role as a commercial center with a new one: warden for the poor.

Is the original function of the city obsolete or does Milwaukee now meet some other needs? Can cities that were born of material necessity become spiritual centers? Is Milwaukee still vital to our future?

We asked a broad range of people—from suburban mayors to city café owners—these questions and were often surprised by the intensity of their responses. Whether you love it or hate it, the city is hard to avoid thinking about; the very concept behind it seems to court controversy. Why do we need Milwaukee? Maybe we don't. But why, then, are there so many answers to the question?

"Obviously, people have a need for some kind of larger entity like the city or they wouldn't congregate around places they are supposedly fleeing. And they don't leave very far."

  - C.J. Hribal, novelist and English professor, Marquette University

"We need a social center. We are social beings and can live in isolation only so long."
- *Margaret Farrow, State Senator (R-Elm Grove)*

"I just got back from four years in California. I was 45 miles from L.A. in a vast, empty suburb. I thought I would go out of my mind."
- *Kate Davy, former Dean of Fine Arts, UW-Milwaukee (She is now Provost and Senior Vice President at Adelphi University, Garden City, New York.)*

"People are hungering for more human contact. Humans need a critical mass of themselves to create enough energy to satisfy our physical and psychological needs."
- *David Kahler, architect*

"If our restaurant was in the suburbs, I don't think we'd have nearly the same charm. Downtown, the tourists and the pedestrian traffic allow for a huge diversity of characters."
- *Larry Krueger, longtime Milwaukee restaurant owner*

"Our neighborhoods have been homogenized to the point where we don't have that cultural and ethnic diversity."
- *Kathryn Bloomberg, Mayor of Brookfield*

"Milwaukee has an excellent ecumenical environment. That means the Episcopal, the Lutheran, the Presbyterian, the Jew … we all meet at least once a month and we just take it for granted that we work together."
- *Archbishop Rembert Weakland*

"I don't think that living in a diverse culture is something most people think about. I think their concerns are more fundamental—am I safe, are the schools okay, what about the taxes, can I park my car?"
- *Mark Belling, WISN Radio talk show host*

"I lived in Milwaukee a couple years. My car got broken into. My brother lives on 17th and Wells and it bothers me no end. Whenever I talk to him on the phone, I hear sirens in the background."
- *James Moriarity, resident and former Mayor of Mequon*

"If you go to certain suburbs, like Mequon, virtually everyone's a doctor or lawyer. Suburban experience is very homogenous—economically, racially, educationally. You get a limited view; it's an unnatural way of looking at life."
- *Christopher Goldsmith, Executive Director, Milwaukee Art Museum*

"I grew up in a seminary. One of the most unhealthy aspects was it was a closed community, where everybody thought the same. You can't close the doors of a city."
- *Ramon Wagner, Executive Director, Community Advocates*

"I remember growing up around cracked pavement… playing really rough and falling on the concrete. I think when kids are too protected, they're afraid to go anywhere else. Things are too safe for them. I don't think you learn as much."
  - Portia Cobb, Associate Professor of Film, UW-Milwaukee

"I know Milwaukee's not what it used to be. But I think about what this city meant to me when I grew up. I gained an education, developed lifelong friendships, learned certain values like hard work from all kinds of people. I remember what it was like to go over to the playground and have to deal with different kinds of people and situations … I still like to watch kids play basketball on the playground."
  - Howard Fuller, Director of Marquette University's Institute for Transformation of Learning.

"There is an efficiency to having a strong downtown. The banks, the law firms, the accountants, the merchants are all together. Many of Northwestern Mutual's critical business partners and advisers are across the Avenue or a few blocks down the street. No technology replaces eyeball-to-eyeball contact…. Face-to-face communication is becoming more crucial to human commerce, not less so."
  - James Ericson, Northwestern Mutual Life CEO

"When it's easier to send electronic messages, you send more. But computers didn't reduce, rather they increased the amount of paper in the office. Electronics may make real face-to-face communication more important. And real cities will have more value."
  - Larry Witzling, Associate Dean of Architecture and Urban Planning Department, UW-Milwaukee

"There's a synergy that happens when you have lots of people in different disciplines together in one location. In New York, once some of the major corporations moved to suburbs and New Jersey, they became ivory tower institutions. The workers became more self-absorbed about the company, rather than how it related to the world. It caused problems in terms of anticipating what customers wanted. Their corporate cultures became very introspective and not very successful."
  - Christopher Goldsmith

"When you have everything spread in exurbia, you lose culture because there's no density and no center. There's no interaction between institutions and people."
  - Polly Morris, Danceworks

"Culture emerges out of congestion and random meetings…the opportunity to see and experience strange things."
  - Jim Shields, architect

"There is a certain creativity that comes from people caged together like rats."
  - Scott Johnson, tavern and restaurant owner

"Living in the city offers so many coincidences, so many meetings. You get a feeling after awhile that every meeting is important, everything you say to people on the street, all the telephone calls, everything. I have in a city so much more of a sense of group consciousness than I do out in the country. With that comes this sense one can use one's tiny weight to influence it, for good or ill. That is why all these meetings are important. You can be part of this organism."
- *Susan Engberg, fiction writer*

"You're not going to eat good Middle Eastern food in the suburbs. You won't see any movies that aren't the top moneymakers that week."
- *Kevin Stallheim, Artistic Director, Present Music*

"It is not a coincidence that the root word for cities, civitas, is the root word for civilization. If you did not have cities, you wouldn't have civilization."
- *David Riemer, head of Milwaukee Department of Administration*

"There seems to be a breakdown of the civility in cities. Part of it might be the rising crime rate, illegitimacy, the breakdown of the family. All of these are ominous indicators of the breakup of the associational brilliance of American life. Without a sense of mutual obligation to people with whom we share the same space, it is not at all clear that we can have the idea of cities as we have known them."
- *Michael Joyce, President, Lynde and Harry Bradley Foundation*

"Waukesha County's marketing identity is inextricably linked to Milwaukee. We would have very little identity without Milwaukee…Even Detroit is still vitally important to its surrounding area. You fly to Detroit, it's not the Pontiac airport you fly to when you're going there."
- *Dan Finley, Waukesha County Executive*

"One thing cities are really great for is preserving what little is left of natural and precious agricultural space. As far as I know, Brookfield used their last brook and field last year."
- *Jim Shields*

Bruce Murphy is a Milwaukee writer and consultant. He is the former editor of the weekly newspaper, *Metro*, and former senior editor of *Milwaukee Magazine*. Tom Bamberger has been the curator of photography at the Milwaukee Art Museum for 10 years. During that time he has curated more than 20 publications. Mr. Bamberger gained an international reputation for creating the first North American museum exhibition and publication for the German artists Anna & Berhard Blume and Andreas Gursky. Mr. Bamberger has also been responsible for building the museum's collections of photographs.

harvey m. jacobs

I received the request to prepare this essay while living in Italy during the Spring of 1999, where I was teaching in UW-Madison's study abroad program. While living in and around Florence I also visited Rome, Venice, Bologna, Pisa and many of the ancient cities of the Tuscan region—Lucca, Siena, Fiesole and Cortona. As I teach urban planning, my residency led me to continuously ponder the nature of cities and community life, the interaction between these two, and to reflect back upon Wisconsin.

Does Wisconsin have real cities? Is Madison a real city? I don't think so. Madison is a conglomeration of people living together in a legally defined place, but there is not much of it that functions as a city, in the way cities were invented and meant to be.

This is not surprising; in the early years of this country's founding, people left Europe to come to America for access to land. Owning a piece of land that you controlled—farming it, planting trees on it, hunting and fishing on it – this is what the American Dream is founded on. Later, in the 19th century migrations that settled Wisconsin, people left Europe and the eastern states for the same reason. (Upstate New York, where many early Wisconsin settlers came from, was believed to be too crowded.)

Americans are profoundly ambivalent about cities and urban-ness. To most Americans, cities are places of danger, crime and chaos. They are places where you confront the unknown—the unknown place, the unknown person, the unknown culture. It is instead in the small towns, the farmstead, the frontier settlement and settler that you find virtue, honesty and those characteristics that best embody that which is American. We seem to have always felt this way—our literature is replete with testimonies to this dichotomy. Our nationally recognized Wisconsin literature? Laura Ingalls Wilder's *Little House on the Prairie* series; Aldo Leopold's *A Sand County Almanac.*

To Europeans, cities denote urbanity, civilization and rising above the parochialness of the countryside—Karl Marx wrote about the idiocy of country life. The European city is density and intensity. It is a mixing of social classes and races. It is an intimacy of neighborhood—knowing the person who sells you the newspaper, knowing your baker, your cheese merchant and your coffee shop attendants. And yet at the same time, the city is the place of random chance and opportunity: not quite knowing who you will meet on the street, who or what will be around the corner or down the path that you have never traveled before. Cities, as Italians invented them in the early part of the second millennium, present one with a paradox—they offer both intimacy and anonymity. You have an innate sense of familiarity in your neighborhood (your village), and yet the city as a whole presents you with the opportunity to become lost, to discover yourself anew by discovering new places and new people.

But above all, the classical city as it was invented, is a place of public life—surrounding you in the squares and cafes from morning into the night. Why? One reason has to do with the unavailability of space. By American and Wisconsin standards, European and Italian homes are small. Physical space is scarcer and thus more valuable. More Europeans live in apartments rather than freestanding homes. If they are fortunate, they have a terrace for some plants and a little outside seating and, if they live on the ground floor, perhaps a small yard. But the majority does not have their own yard, garden or children's play area. By contrast, Wisconsinites share the American desire for private land and personal space. We retreat into our home spaces; we are captured and perhaps isolated by them. We covet our small pieces of land, reflecting the reason many of our ancestors came to America. But the consequence of this use and arrangement of space is that we are private consumers.

In contrast, Italians are public consumers. They enjoy and take pride in the privacy of their homes as much as anyone anywhere, but an essential part of their lives includes time spent shared with their community. Each evening, from about 5 p.m. to 7 p.m., people of all ages take an evening walk in their neighborhood—known as the passeggiata. People stop and talk, young people eye each other, older people admire and watch over the teenagers, everyone enjoys the babies and toddlers. And everyone gets a public education by watching everyone else—children learn how to grow into young people, young people into adults, adults into older adults and older adults learn about today's youth culture.

Beyond the passeggiata, Italians make full use of the squares that are the hubs of their cities. The fruit and vegetable markets, the clothing markets, the antique and resale markets all happen in the squares and give people a further opportunity to undertake the business of life together. Concerts, fairs, plays—spettacolo to the Italians—take place in the square, with ready access for all, from the family with children in strollers to the homeless.

Anticipating an accusation that I am over-romanticizing life in Italy, let me be clear about my point—Italians create the city by living in it fully, by engaging in it, by making it their place.

How does all this relate to Madison? Why am I arguing that Madison isn't a city? Perhaps most fundamentally, because many of Madison's residents actively and enthusiastically abandon the city. What characterizes Madison? The Capitol Square is the symbol of the city, sitting as it does in the center of the Isthmus. But what really characterizes Madison is the growth of its suburbs, on both sides of the isthmus. Madison has undergone a social transformation to a population that has no relationship to its public spaces.

Several years ago, I was shopping in a store in a nondescript mall on the West Side. It was the winter holiday season. I mentioned to the clerk that I was going to the Civic Center that weekend for the annual performance of The Nutcracker, as my daughter was dancing in it. She paused and then said, "You know, I don't think I have been downtown for six or seven years." We were five miles from the Civic Center. I wish this was an isolated instance, but it isn't.

Wisconsin used to have cities. Milwaukee was a city. Madison was a city. There were vibrant neighborhoods with people who actively engaged the city's public spaces. But for many reasons, including urban renewal, the interstate highway system, white flight and a changed economic structure, the cities that were are no more.

Can Madison become a city? By my definition, it has all the right elements. It has the urban downtown mall of State Street, the Terrace behind the Memorial Union on the UW campus, the Capitol Square (scene of the Farmer's Market, the Art Show, the Taste of Madison and the family New Year's celebration), and now the rooftop of the new Convention Center. And these are only our grand public spaces. The city is full of small parks and other places to gather. All of these are admirable and engaging public spaces, with tremendous potential to bring people together, which they do on occasion, but not with regularity.

People have to want to be brought together. They have to enjoy it; they have to embrace the excitement, the vitality, the familiarity and the uncertainty of interacting in a public space. My experience, my reflection, is that for the most part, most people, most of the time, don't want it. It saddens me, because I believe we would all be enriched by it. So for now, all I can do is encourage you to join me in searching for, and helping to create, urban Wisconsin.

Harvey M. Jacobs is a professor at the University of Wisconsin-Madison, where he teaches in the Department of Urban and Regional Planning and the Institute for Environmental Studies, and serves as director of the Land Tenure Center, a research, technical assistance and training institute. In 1998, the University of Wisconsin Press published his book *Who Owns America? Social Conflict Over Property Rights*.

henry h. smith milwaukee's coastline at night

epilogue

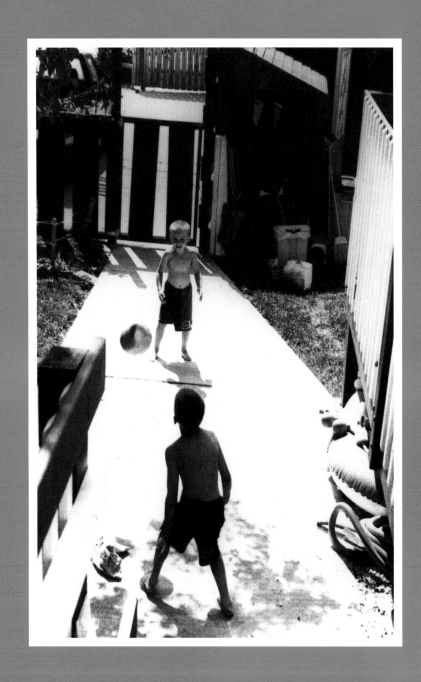

ryan heckel a summer day

the old neighborhood

ray suarez

One of the most popular motifs in today's press is that Americans are searching for community, searching for meaning in their lives, hunting for something they know is missing, if only they knew what it was. The assumptions aren't questioned very strenuously, because they act as the framework for the story. The journalists don't dig to that second level of analysis that might expose uncomfortable truths about the places people live, where the dissatisfaction festers, where it seems so hard to find community.

Humans are social beings. However, much of America's residential construction takes no account of that, and puts too much pressure on the nuclear family to provide for all our emotional needs. We share the road but little else...we walk directly into the car from our home, moving from one private realm into another. We keep far apart, wrapped in a personal realm of glass and steel, rubber and plastic, and embrace a system that prefers to see us as consumers, instead of as citizens.

We continue to artificially separate the functions of our lives...family, social, commercial, spiritual, making sure zoning laws force these different roles into different physical realms. As a person who walks his children to school...takes a train to work...walks to church...grabs milk and bread and juice on the way home from the train, I find this other kind of life mysterious. I imagine it to be totally lacking in appeal for many of the people who live it, but who are convinced they have no choice.

In the old, pre-automania landscape, there were public places of spectacle, gathering, ritual. They were paid for by us all, and used for the defining moments of shared civic life. Today the landscape is privatized, so many of those same functions once carried on in a public realm, now are instead done in privatized, controlled space, patrolled by private security forces. The mall is not main street or the courthouse square, a bookstore is not a public library, a health club is not a public park, a private school is not a public school, and a private automobile is not a street car. Outwardly, those old, public realms performed many of the same functions of the new, privatized realms. But at base their missions, their reasons for being, were totally different.

We are a much richer society than we were fifty, sixty and seventy years ago when many of the old neighborhoods were being built, and rebuilt. So, if we headed back to the denser, more efficient and more humane environment of the old neighborhood, we wouldn't build it the same way. You wouldn't have to live the way your grandmother lived. My first apartment, a $150-a-month beauty on the Lower East Side of Manhattan, had a tub in the kitchen and a toilet in a spare closet. No one's saying that we must live the way urbanites did before the Second World War. People who are moving to brand spanking new housing in the Bronx, and East Cleveland, and just south of the loop in Chicago don't live in cramped tenements, or put on a robe to head down the hall to the common bathroom.

People who say, "I don't want to live that life again" are giving a negative response to a question no one is even asking. The old neighborhood was shaped by economic and social necessities. And it was a product of its time, and a country where the per capita incomes in adjusted dollars were less than half what they are now. If Americans rediscover this internal New Frontier, it will be a place built to respond to the economic and social realities of today.

Cities, homes, factories, warehouses, retail districts, all express what the city was for in the first place. It is an agglomeration of capital, a place where buyers meet sellers, where workers meet employers, where people involved in a myriad of enterprises find a concentration of the talent and creativity that allows capital to find its highest and best use.

Today, when you travel to any city, you'll find vast stretches of capital. Abandoned houses, empty warehouses, collapsing factories, that were once worth huge amounts of money, places that spun off the profits that produced taxes and wages and supported schools and generation after generation's ascent into the middle class.

Thousands of acres of these places are in ruin. Did they change intrinsically? Did people stop needing places to live? Did people stop needing steel, or workers stop needing jobs? When these built places were not living up to the desires we had for them, we left them behind, and started from scratch somewhere else. But unlike a part of nature that can return to a wild state when the hand of man no longer changes it, cities don't return to the bush. We are not like nomads who leave a place and thus remove the pressure of human habitation. Unused parts of the urban landscape don't become forest or wilderness when we don't love them any more. Nope, these places keep forcing an obligation on municipal governments, they keep leaching heavy metals into the soil, they keep a claim on the land, while producing no wealth for the society.

But, we put these places behind us, and start fresh messing up some new place. This is not a left-right issue, a conservative-liberal issue, a Republican-Democrat issue. It is none of these things. If we really were capitalists, people would be coming back to the city in droves, because housing is getting cheaper, land is getting cheaper, even industrial and commercial investment is getting cheaper. Offer the efficiencies of rail, highway and air cargo access, connection to major municipal water systems—an infrastructure is already in place. If we really were capitalists, some of those jobs running to the development perimeter where the new communities are, would instead be heading back toward the center, where we don't need to wait for new workers to move in, they're already here. So there is something else at work besides the desire to optimize the use of capital, make a buck, seize an opportunity.

Are the cities back? Does being back mean that lots of your citizens are getting newly created jobs? Does being back mean that people with jobs and aspirations of owning a home are moving into your city? What does being back mean when the economic and residential heart of your metropolitan area is home to a smaller and smaller portion of the residents, and a smaller and smaller portion of the jobs?

Crime is down. Job creation is up. Some of the most glaring problems of urban America are finally being addressed just as some cities come dangerously close to the point of no return. A few new downtown employers, a downtown people-mover, or a fancy new atrium hotel can't hide an increasingly obvious trend: suburban America is growing increasingly comfortable using the city—for employment, entertainment, education—but will not move in. Many cities are so desperate for economic activity that they can't be too fussy about that difficult truth. For now, the thinking goes, let's get them in here and spending money for as many hours as we can manage, before they head home over the city line. But hungry cities acting as the entertainer, the court jester for suburban America just doesn't go far enough. A resident, in a thousand little ways, spins off economic activity unmatched by the casual visitor who visits your attraction, watches a movie, buys a T-shirt and a frozen yogurt, and heads home.

Why do so many interests continue to build on virgin ground, or some of the finest farmland in North America? Why do people pull out of depopulating school districts only to demand new schools in that place where they arrive? Why do they sit on choked suburban arterial streets in traffic moving three to five miles an hour, until they can amass the political clout behind new road construction?

Because so many of the costs are shifted such that further sprawl seems like an economically rational act. Do new homeowners in subdivisions pay an increased tax to make up for the municipal costs that come from flash flooding because there is no longer sufficient unimpeded drainage in low-lying areas? Do they pay higher cable bills for the added costs of being hooked up to the grid? Higher phone bills? More income taxes to support the Defense Department, which spends billions patrolling the Persian Gulf in order to satisfy their gasoline habit? Do you get a check from an upwind auto-dependent community for what they're doing to your air by using the car for literally every errand, every social transaction that life demands? The short answer is of course, no. And sprawl remains economically rational behavior because of the web of subsidies great and small that continue to drive people further and further away from the historic urban core, rather than back into the increasingly appealing center.

Any attempt to talk about the social costs of one of the primary contributors to sprawl—the automobile—is shouted down, we just don't want to know. We must make believe, for the purposes of having any conversation, that the auto must be given its pride of place as the lowest cost, highest efficiency mover of people in every circumstance. This is not just a matter of environmental concern...or economic concern. What are we doing to ourselves by building communities the way we do?

I recently interviewed one suburban St. Louis couple, now retired, both man and wife grew up in the city limits and became part of the exodus to St. Louis County in the 1960s. The wife said she never felt as lonely as when she was waiting for cataract surgery just before her husband quit full-time work. No longer able to drive, and with virtually nothing but other homes within walking distance, she sat in the house, with a TV she couldn't really see for company. It got her thinking about what life would be like twenty years from now, when instead of being a relatively mobile 65, she would be, God willing, 85. Would she still want to take the car everywhere she needed to go? How easy would it be, in such a dispersed landscape, to hook up with people who share her interests, how would they find each other, and how would they spend their day?

Let me suggest that the human ecology of sprawl creates a hostile environment for children as well. Changes, not only in the way we organize space, but in the way we organize our daily lives, mean that childhood is a radically different proposition for tens of millions of American children than it was when I was a child. The ability to learn self-reliance is being sucked out of childhood by adult fear of unsupervised time in many places. We are afraid to let children take public buses, or head to the next town on their bikes. I talk to parents who are afraid of simply letting their children play in the streets of their community, or travel on their own. More and more families have both adults working, commutes are longer, and so our children must spend more hours in institutional settings...or behind closed doors at home until mom and dad come home.

These children are bored, prone to trouble, unable to learn the skills of self-reliance that come with managing your time in the realms of childhood...the public park, the streets and stores of the neighborhood. There is no neighborhood, there are collections of homes. No wonder teenagers are dying to drive at younger and younger ages, and no wonder we let them. In order to keep them safe from the media-generated images of dangerous streets and dangerous transportation, we nervously put them in the most dangerous place a young teenager can be...behind the wheel of a car.

So, if the new world being built at the furthest edge of today's metropolitan area isn't working for us socially; and it is defying the laws of capitalist economics; and it is environmentally irrational to continue to lay out new oceans of asphalt and labyrinths of cul de sacs; then why do we do it?

Zoning is one answer. Force of habit is another. The U.S. tax code is another. Race is a potent shaper of the human landscape. Fear of crime and fear of public schools are part of it. And the tempting possibilities of responsibility and cost-free waste closes the sale. It is the tragedy of the commons writ large...what is smart for me isn't great for everybody. If we move to cut down on automobile dependence for commuting, the big winner is the guy who's going to keep on driving no matter what, all we'll succeed in is making that guy's commute happier and shorter. His individual utility is served by everyone else's sacrifices.

I am, ultimately, an optimist. I hope that we can get away from defining these issues in a partisan or left-right way. Wanting to live in community is not a left-wing issue. Some of the hardest right right-wingers in America have gone off into the interior of the country to build towns and counties where they can live lives that make sense to them, where they can live according to their beliefs.

But we've got to see ourselves plain for this to work. We've got to admit that the road to urban decay was paved, not with good intentions, but with alibis. That by exalting individual convenience to the status of a new national religion, we have built ourselves metropolitan areas that duplicate services, are dirty and wasteful, and don't make everyone happy. Why are we so intent on clinging to this life when, when other people aren't around, we complain to high heaven about the way things are? Let's be honest about how things got the way they are, and how we're going to fix them.

Note: The following is an excerpt of a speech Mr. Suarez delivered at a 1000 Friends of Wisconsin event in the Spring of 1999.

Ray Suarez is the former host of National Public Radio's "Talk of the Nation." He can currently be seen nightly on "The News Hour with Jim Lehrer" on PBS. His recently published book, *The Old Neighborhood: What We Lost in the Great Suburban Migration*, has received national acclaim.

about the photographers, artists and artwork

Tom Bamberger has been the curator of photography at the Milwaukee Art Museum for 10 years. During that time he has curated more than 40 exhibitions and produced more than 20 publications. Mr. Bamberger has gained an international reputation for creating the first North American museum exhibition and publication for the German artists Anna & Berhard Blume and Andreas Gursky. Mr. Bamberger has also been responsible for building the museum's collection of photographs. The "Girl Engaged in Street Painting" photo was originally published in the *Milwaukee Magazine's City Guide '98*.

Student photographer **Ryan Heckel**, a 19-year-old Milwaukee native, graduated from Rufus King High School in 1999 and now attends the University of Wisconsin-Madison.

Tim Holte has lived and worked in Milwaukee for 25 years. His work has appeared in *Art Muscle* (a former Milwaukee-based arts magazine), and was recently selected for inclusion in an exhibit featuring 4-inch-by-6-inch postcard art at the John Michael Kohler Arts Center.

The **SC Johnson** Administration Building's Great Workroom was designed by Frank Lloyd Wright to meet the needs of SC Johnson following his study of the flow of business and functions of the company and employees. The support of dendriform columns—designed on the premise of a flower with its stem, calyx and petals—adds greater structural strength, beauty and floor space equaling nearly one half-acre. SC Johnson's international head-quarters is called the "center of creativity," and the buildings have garnered numerous architectural awards. SC Johnson is a 114-year-old family-owned and managed company with a strong commitment to innovation, work-place excellence and community/environmental leadership. (Photograph courtesy of SC Johnson.)

Student photographer **Thairath Khanthavong** won an award for his photograph, "Curious Joe," while attending Washington High School in Milwaukee.

Student photographer **Colin Kloecher**, 17, grew up in Milwaukee and currently attends the Milwaukee High School of the Arts where he is majoring in visual arts.

Ned Luhm, a member of the League of Milwaukee Artists, is a multi-media artist whose work can be seen in cafés and galleries around Milwaukee.

Brent Nicastro is one of Wisconsin's most prolific photographers. He has been practicing his art for more than two decades, and his work has appeared in hundreds of publications around the world including *On Wisconsin*, *TIME*, *People*, *Money*, *USA Today*, and *Parade*, as well as in many other newspapers, textbooks, calendars and trade publications. His most recent book of photography, *Madison*, captures the city, its people, their activities and the natural beauty of the isthmus-city in 100 full-color photographs.

Matt Nolen has taught, juried and lectured widely and has been Adjunct Professor of Art at New York University, since 1991. He has received numerous awards and honors including a New York Foundation for the Arts Artists' Fellowship and a Mid-Atlantic Arts Foundation/NEW Regional Fellowship. He executed his "The Social History of Architecture" project of hand-painted and glazed tiles, toilets, lavatories and urinals between August 2 and December 4, 1999.

Henry H. Smith, photographer, instructor and lab wizard, relishes the urban experience offered by his native city, Milwaukee. Capturing the city as it re-invents itself is an ongoing personal assignment for him. His photography and Japanese calligraphy are exhibited primarily in southeastern Wisconsin.

Mary Jo Walicki graduated from Madison Area Technical College with Associate Degrees in Photography and Horticulture & Landscape Design. She is currently a photographer for the Milwaukee Journal Sentinel, and her freelance photography has been published by *Sports Illustrated, People* and *USA Today*, among other publications.

Zane Williams has been photographing Wisconsin for nearly thirty years. His color images portraying the land, the people and the culture of the state were published in *Wisconsin*, by Graphic Arts Center Publishing, which is now in its third printing. Most recently, his four-year project re-photographing over 120 historic views of the city of Madison has been accepted by the University of Wisconsin Press for publication in the fall of 2001. Zane lives with his wife Mary in a historic home a few blocks from the Capitol Square in downtown Madison.